Fishing

Yellowstone

Waters

Fishing

Yellowstone

Waters

Charles E. Brooks

Photographs by Dan Callaghan

Nick Lyons Books

NICK LYONS BOOKS
31 W 21 Street
New York, NY 10010

PRINTED IN THE UNITED STATES OF AMERICA
10 9 8 7 6 5 4

Designed by Tasha Hall

Library of Congress Cataloging in Publication Data

Brooks, Charles E., 1921-
    Fishing Yellowstone waters.

    Includes index.
    1. Fishing—Yellowstone National Park. I. Title.
SH464.Y45B76   1984   799.1'1'0978752   83-23765
ISBN 1-55821-017-2

To Howard Back and Roderick Haig-Brown,
who loved rivers and wrote beautifully about them,
from Dan and Charlie,
who love their work.

Contents

Yellowstone Waters 9

1   General Information 13

2   Gardner River 19

3   Slough Creek 27

4   Lamar River 35

5   Lewis River 43

6   Firehole River 53

7   Gibbon River 69

8   Madison River 77

9   Gallatin River 99

10   Henry's Fork, Snake River 109

11   Yellowstone River 123

Photographer's Notes 135

Appendixes 145

Bibliography 155

Index 157

Second Meadow at Slough Creek. Angler—Craig Mathews.

Yellowstone Waters

The area within a two-hour drive of West Yellowstone, Montana, contains about 2,000 miles of trout streams. About 1,000 of those miles lie within Yellowstone Park itself, and 90 percent of all these stream miles, in the Park and out, are public waters.

There is no area in this country, or any other, that contains as many good trout streams in so small a space of miles or which are so easily reached. A good portion of those trout stream miles lie adjacent to, or only a brief distance from, major highways or other good roads. The Yellowstone, Firehole, Gibbon, Madison, Gallatin, Gardner and Lamar rivers all bring joy to the angler by having most of their best stretches running beside good roads. The Henry's Fork from Henry's Lake to the campground at Riverside, is paralleled by U.S. 191, the major highway crossing the area.

Only the Yellowstone River above the lake, the Lewis River and Slough Creek, of the streams covered herein, are difficult to reach in their better stretches. That does not necessarily mean that they are the better fishing. The astonishing thing about this area is that there are many stretches of stream that actually can be, and have been, fished by persons confined to wheelchairs, and these stretches, in some cases, are among the best fishing spots on the entire river. I have caught three-pound trout on these rivers in spots where I have also hooked, on my back cast, a car driving by.

There is another thing about these streams to gladden the heart of the fisherman, conservationist and ecologist. They are being better managed, both for protection of the environment, and as a quality fishery, than any streams in the world. Many of the practices pioneered here to create a quality fishing experience are now widely accepted elsewhere. The fishing in some of the streams has dramatically improved over the past ten years and this will be a continuing thing.

Stocking of trout in Yellowstone Park streams was discontinued in the late 1950s. The environment there has been protected almost since it was discovered by white men. Except for "improvements" to allow the 2.5 million yearly visitors better access to the natural wonders—mostly geyser basins and the Grand Canyon of the Yellowstone—the area has been unharmed, the watersheds completely undamaged. The streams run as clear and pure now as they did 200 years ago, before the white men came. Yellowstone Park is an area of wild rivers containing wild trout, which are both plentiful and large. And under the present enlightened management procedures, it will remain that way.

In the early 1970s, the Fish and Game Department of the state of Montana also stopped the stocking of hatchery trout in good naturally producing streams. About the same time, state and county officials began a serious attempt to protect the environment and to repair, where possible, damages from past undesirable practices.

Both Yellowstone Park and Montana officials are agreed on two things: that fishing is the largest single recreational industry in this nation, and that most of this nation's 50 million fishermen are also strong environmentalists.

Idaho only recently had become aware of the economic benefits that fishermen bring to any area they visit in numbers, and has also begun programs to protect the environment and to produce or maintain quality fisheries. It is no coincidence that the first area in which this state moved to improve a trout fishery was adjacent to both Yellowstone Park and southwestern Montana. The Henry's Fork just may be, for size and numbers of wild trout, the finest trout stream in the United States.

Both states and Yellowstone Park have come to use harvest numbers as one way to maintain a quality fishery. Therefore one will find in this area a limit (or no-kill) regulation that varies not only by stream but by stretch of stream. Yet for the angler fishing for a trout supper, there are plenty of available streams.

The environs of trout streams are invariably beautiful, and the varied beauties of this area are the equal of any. The Park, once a series of volcanic calderas, for the most part, is the mother of mighty rivers. The headwaters of the Madison, Yellowstone, Snake and Gallatin all lie in these majestic uplands. There is no area of the Rocky Mountain better watered or more beautiful.

The mountain ranges, towering almost to 12,000 feet, flank the collapsed and lava-filled calderas. The Beartooth on the north is one of the most spectacular of ranges, as is the Absaroka on the east, of which the Beartooth Range is a part. On the south is the grandeur of the Tetons, on the west are the Henry's Lake, Madison and Gallatin ranges. The ice- and snow-covered slopes of these ranges provide a never-failing source of cold, clear, mineral- and oxygen-rich water, which is ideal for trout and trout stream insects. The interior elevation of the Park averages 6,500 feet exclusive of the mountain ranges themselves, and even the lower reaches of these streams, after they depart the Park, are a mile or more above sea level.

The forests that blanket the region have suffered no damage from man or fire in the

Park; and without, the ill effects of overtimbering are either few or have been overcome by the healing hand of time. Overgrazing, endemic in the West, has been brought under control in the southwestern Montana and Idaho watersheds, and beneficial land-use practices are everywhere in effect.

The trout—rainbow, brown, brook, cutthroat and even lake trout—are being treated as a treasure, which in fact, they are.

This is the greatest trout-fishing paradise anywhere on this earth and its future is brighter today than it was ten years ago; ten years from now it will be better still. And most of it will be ours to enjoy forever.

Near Rockhaven on the Gallatin River.

1
General Information

The size of the area included in this book will surprise a great number of people, especially those from smaller states. Though all the streams mentioned herein are within an easy two-hour drive from West Yellowstone, the area encompassed is huge.

Yellowstone Park alone comprises more than 3,400 square miles, or 2.2 million acres. It is larger than the states of Delaware, Rhode Island *and* the District of Columbia combined. When the area encompassing the Madison from the Park boundary to Ennis, and the Henry's Fork from the continental divide to Riverside Campground is included, we have added an additional 8,000 square miles of area to that of the Park.

Fortunately for the prospective angler, the entire area is dedicated to serving the visitor. Accommodations of every kind exist throughout the area: West Yellowstone alone can bed down—in motels, hotels, R.V. parks, and campgrounds—about 8,000 people a night.

For the nonangling members of one's family, there are many things to see and do; sight-seeing, horseback riding, water-skiing and boating, nature trips, photographic opportunities, museums, art galleries, theaters—both stage and movie—and, of course, bars and nightclubs.

For the angler, other considerations aside, the decision of where to stay, so as not to waste precious fishing time, is not critical. Only one of the areas is located several hours away: The upper Yellowstone River must be reached by horseback, hiking or by power *and* paddled watercraft. No matter where one stays, it takes at least a half-day to reach this area.

The Gallatin can be reached by its upper section by a thirty-minute drive from West

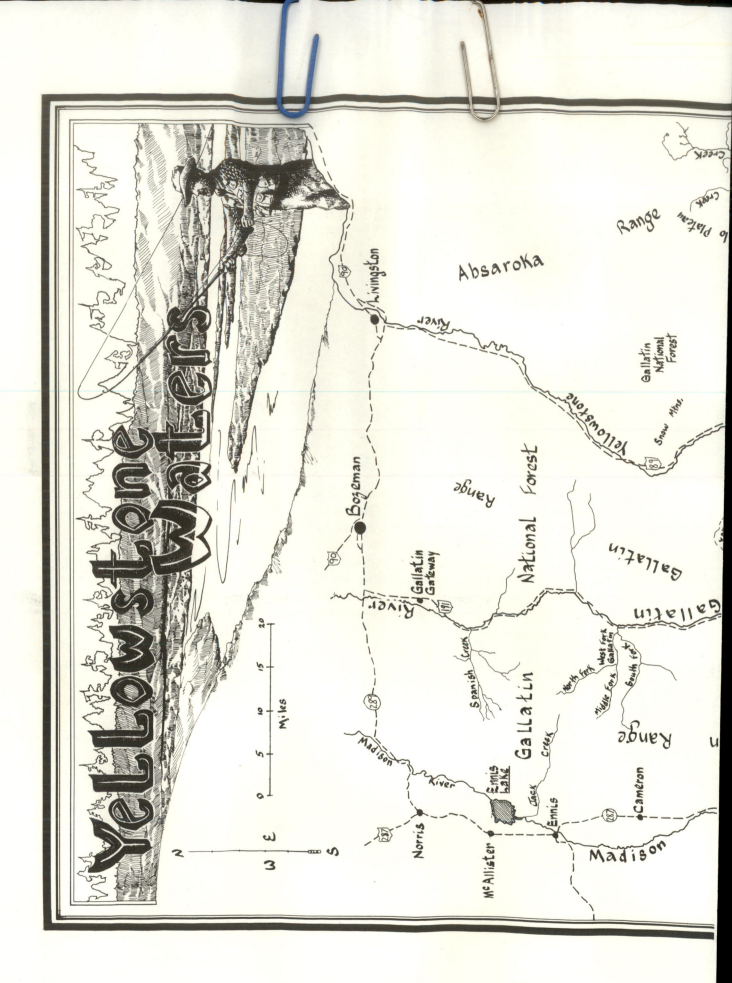

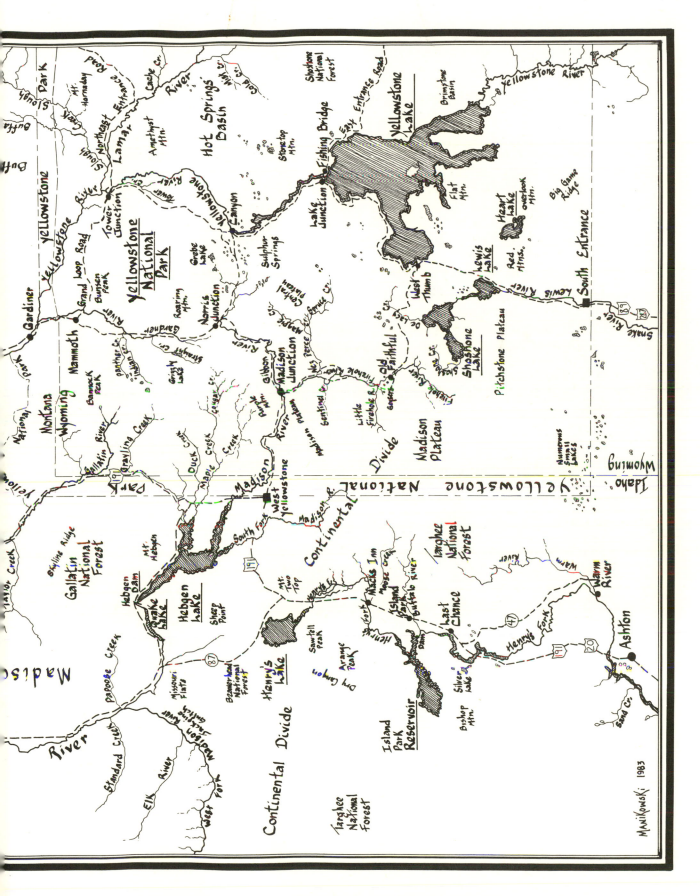

Manikowski 1983

Yellowstone. The middle section is a few minutes from Karst's Ranch, and the lower section of our coverage ends at Gallatin Gateway.

The Gardner is best covered from the town of Gardiner on the Yellowstone (the name of the town is not spelled the same as the river and they are unconnected in history). For the camper, there are places to camp near Park Headquarters at Mammoth and in Gardner's Hole. The Park Historical Museum and Library at Mammoth are very much worth a visit.

Slough Creek can best be reached either from Gardiner, Tower Junction in the Park, or Cooke City at its northeast entrance; the Lamar is best covered from these places also.

The Lewis can be reached most easily from its own campground on Lewis Lake. Quarters are available at Grant Village and West Thumb, both in easy driving distance.

One can get to the upper Gibbon in about the same time from Canyon or Madison Junction, but there is only a campground, no quarters, at the latter.

The Firehole has Old Faithful Inn and Lodge at its upper end and Madison Junction Campground at its lower.

The Yellowstone, of which nearly a hundred miles are considered herein, can be reached at its different sections from eight stations (in order from the south): Grant Village, West Thumb, Lake, Fishing Bridge, Canyon, Tower Junction, Mammoth and Gardiner. It should be noted that a revamping of the Park's visitor accommodations is currently under way; some of these areas are being upgraded with motellike quarters, some downgraded to camping only, others may be eliminated for overnight stopping.

Coming downstream along the Madison one finds the campground at Madison Junction, West Yellowstone, Baker's Hole, the Hebgen Lake resort area, Slide Inn with its trailer park, West Fork, Cameron and Ennis, with several lesser areas of camping and rustic quarters scattered throughout. The area along the entire length of the Madison is much devoted to caring for the fishermen and his or her family.

Henry's Fork area is also devoted to the fisher and family. Around Henry's Lake are all kinds of arrangements including trailer-R.V. parks, campgrounds, cabins, lodges and so forth. Mack's Inn, where the river crosses the highway for the second time, is strictly a resort area, being located in a portion of Island Park Village, which uses U.S. 191 as a thirty-mile-long main street. Further downstream, one finds camps, resorts and guest ranches to suit the needs of any appetite. Pond's Lodge is ideally located at the Island Park Dam, giving quick access to the reservoir above and Box Canyon below, as well as the tributary Buffalo, a fine, easily waded, gentle trout stream (although mostly a panfishery).

Below Box Canyon is Last Chance, with camping and other accommodations, immediate access to one of the finest trout stream stretches in the entire world, plus Harriman State Park (Railroad Ranch). And at the end of our coverage is the splendidly located campground at Riverside.

All the towns and villages in the entire Yellowstone Waters area are largely places that cater to the angler and family. First-class tackle shops and guide service are everywhere. The competition is such that only the very good, in either guide service or tackle shops, can survive. One has an abundance of choice.

Speaking of tackle, a variety isn't necessary if it's chosen with care. This is big country and subject to strong convection winds in summer, when the cold air on the mountains rushes down to replace warmer air uplifted by heat. Winds of thirty-five to fifty miles per hour are not unusual on our small streams as well as the larger ones. One does not choose tackle here by the size of the stream or the fish, but by the size of the wind.

Generally speaking, a size 7 fly line is as light as one can be certain of using all the time. I've seen proponents of size 4 outfits literally reduced to tears because, during a two-week vacation, they were unable to fish a single day on the stream of their choice because of wind. I will have something to say about flies, natural and artificial, at the end of each chapter. There are local flies which may, at times, be the only thing that works. But most times choice of fly is not that critical.

Choice of clothing is. The area is located between the 44th and 45th parallels of north latitude, and mostly above 6,000 feet. Radiational cooling in the thin air causes large swings in temperature. The July averages at West Yellowstone will be about 78 degrees Fahrenheit in the day and 45 at night. But I have fished here about twenty days a year from 1948 to 1964, and I have lived here since 1964, and I've seen July day temperatures no higher than 40 and nights of 28. I've fished days in mid-July when it was snowing so hard I couldn't see the far bank. West Yellowstone, on more than one occasion, has had eight inches of snow in August. It averages eighteen days of rain during June, and there are heavy thunderstorms circling the area all summer. Warm clothing and rain gear are musts to insure a carefree vacation fishing trip.

Of course, everything one needs can be bought here. But if you have to purchase a thirty-dollar item here that you carelessly or thoughtlessly left at home, it's going to take some of the bloom off your visit.

High waders are a must, as are felt soles. There are a *very* few stretches where hobs or wading chains are nice, but I've never worn them in over 10,000 hours of wading over a hundred streams in this area. If you own a wading staff, bring it. You'll need it. Also, a net—if it's large. You won't need a net for small fish, and you'll invariably find Cotton's Law in effect: When you hook a very large trout, there will be no place to beach it. When I speak of large nets, I'm thinking that in 1982, trout of twenty-four to thirty-three inches were caught in the streams mentioned herein. The fellow that caught the latter had to baby it down a half-mile of boulder-strewn, fast-running stream before he found a place to beach it. By then, he was so tired he had to have help, and was a nervous wreck, besides.

I don't mean to imply that the weather here is always, or even often, bad or that things will always go wrong. But the best way to ruin a vacation or a fishing trip is to start out unprepared. Expect the best but prepare for the worst. That is Charlie's Law.

Obsidian Creek, a tributary to the Gardner.

2
Gardner River

Rising on the northeast slope of Joseph Peak in the northwest corner of Yellowstone Park, the Gardner is first seen by most anglers in Gardner's Hole.

Hole, as a place-name in the West, is a term of varied significance. It is applied to high landlocked basins (Freezeout Hole), to mountain-girt valleys (Jackson's Hole), to desert sinks (Humboldt's Hole) or even to a spot on a river where the water depth increases sharply. Most generally, in the northern Rockies, it refers to a subalpine basin, and that is what Gardner's Hole is. It is surpassingly beautiful.

The river starts as a tiny, icy trickle almost 10,000 feet up. By the time it reaches the northwest corner of Gardner's Hole it has been joined by several other icy small streams but it is not yet fishworthy.

In Gardner's Hole, which it traverses the full length in a northwest-southeast direction, it is joined by Fawn, Panther, Indian and Obsidian creeks, as lovely a quartet of trout stream names as one will find, and the streams are just as lovely.

All are small, winding, willow lined, clear and cold, and all host numbers of brook and rainbow trout. These four streams, and the river here, are the only ones in the Park that may be fished with worms—but only by children twelve years and under. This is a family fishing area, with an excellent campground located near where Panther, Indian and Obsidian creeks join the main river.

The Park administration, in choosing this as a family fishing area, acted with a wisdom not always applied to other aspects under their control. The area abounds with deer, elk, moose, waterfowl, beaver, squirrels, chipmunks and other small creatures, and birds. Opportunities for wildlife photos are everywhere. The area is scenic and the

Water Ouzel.

Marmot, near Sheepeater Cliffs area.

main road just a few hundred yards away.

The fish are mostly panfish size. A rainbow or brookie of a foot or more is a bragging fish. The small, winding streams with their undercut banks and clearly defined deeper spots, are ideal for worm fishing by the beginning angler. The mainstream at the confluence with the other creeks is also largely a panfish proposition. But it is a delight to fish with small wet flies, a high-riding dry fly and, in season (August and September), with a hopper pattern.

From where it passes under the Norris-Mammoth road bridge, there is downstream a mile or so of very pleasant water. But as one proceeds, the walls of the canyon move steadily inward upon the stream, the bed becomes rocky and boulder filled and one is at last forced to proceed almost entirely in the stream if he wishes to continue. In a while, with Bunsen Peak towering over the stream to the north and the abrupt face of Sheepeater Cliffs on the south, the stream becomes a torrent racing for its leap over Osprey Falls, and the even steeper canyon below. It is dangerous to continue.

It returns to a more fishable approach under the soaring bridge on the Mammoth-Tower Junction road. Here one may fish his happy way both up and down stream. It is swift, boulder-filled pocket water, and the fish, somewhat larger than above, are also more plentiful. Lava Creek adds its mineral-rich input just downstream of the road bridge and almost doubles the flow.

The next approach to the river is a dirt road from the newer housing section for Park Headquarters at Mammoth. By using both approaches one can cover the entire area between without walking or wading more than a half-mile. From the housing area road it is another half-mile before the stream comes into sight along the Mammoth-Gardiner road (roads in Yellowstone Park are not numbered but are identified by the names of the areas at either end of a section of road).

The five miles or so of stream in the Mammoth-Gardiner area are very pleasant miles to fish. There is just enough difficulty getting into and out of the stream, and in fishing it, to deter the casual, and the regulations and constant patrol by rangers give pause to the meat fisherman.

It is a prolific piece of water *for the proficient* fly-fisher. The fish are larger than farther up, and there are, now and then, run-up fish from the Yellowstone, which the Gardner joins within the boundary of the town. A knowledgeable fly-fisher *can*, on a good day, take and release fifty or more trout. But he can also get skunked. You must know what you are about to do well in the lower Gardner.

The "salmonfly," really the giant stone fly *Pteronarcys californica*, emerges (hatches, in angler parlance) in June and July. Thus the nymphs of this insect are always in the stream, since it lives there four years from the time the egg is laid until it becomes a flying adult. A large black fly such as a Woolly Worm or one of the nearly two dozen local nymphal imitations will take fish most of the time. These are difficult to fish in this broken, boulder-filled pocket water stream and only the experienced nympher will do well.

Near Mammoth on Gardner River.

My good friends, Sharman and Bob Wilson, who have a summer place in Gardiner, have immense success with the dry fly. But Sharm and Bob are not only very proficient dry fly fishers, they fish the river as much as forty days a season and are completely familiar with it. Still, the visiting angler who is reasonably adept with the dry fly can expect a banner day now and then on this intriguing stream, and a good day most any time.

In September, the big browns will commence to run up the river from the Yellowstone, and when the spawning run is fully under way, this small river will hold an astonishing number of really huge fish. One can see them making their way upstream from many of the pullouts along the Mammoth-Gardiner road, but the best spots to watch from are those overlooking the Rifle Rapids—Shotgun Chute stretch (these are angler's names, not official Park names. Rangers will not know them by these names).

I have watched five- and six-pound browns leaping the cascades in this area, looking more like salmon than brown trout. The Park Service has closed to fishing certain of these areas in spawning time, although they may be fished during the rest of the season. But areas above and below are open, and anytime during the run-up one may hook into a really large trout that will, in all probability, "clean" the angler on a slashing, dodging, rock-hopping run back to the Yellowstone, leaving him with an empty reel, a broken leader and well-barked shins. But it's a glorious experience and shouldn't be missed. It's one of the reasons that the fall is my favorite time on the Gardner.

NATURALS AND ARTIFICIALS

The upper Gardner above Osprey Falls hosts *mostly* small insects. Still, large dry flies work well. Royal Wulff, Goofus Bug and Hair Wing Variant in sizes 10 and 12 are good most anytime. More imitative flies such as Blue Dun in 14 and 16, Light Cahill in the same sizes and the Adams will fill the bill for mayfly types. But the Gardner, and most other streams in this area, host more caddis types than mayfly.

The Elk Hair Caddis, Colorado King and Goddard Caddis are most used. Sizes 12, 14 and 16, in gray and in brown will cover nearly all caddis hatches. The few small stone flies here will be well enough matched by these patterns. Hopper patterns from mid-July onward are a must.

The lower river hosts the big stone flies, and one needs the big black nymphs, Bitch Creek, Montana Nymph or any one of over twenty local patterns in sizes 6 and 4, both 4XL. During the salmonfly emergence in June, Sofa Pillow, Bird's Stonefly or Parks'

Salmon Fly in the same sizes will handle this hatch, and the flies used in the upper section work here also.

For wet flies a selection of soft hackles in sizes 10 and 12, Grey Hackle, Grouse and Green, Partridge and Orange, Carey Special and a wet Coachman will take care of most situations.

In the upper river one will not find the trout unduly selective, but the lower river requires much closer attention in obtaining the proper fly, as well as in its use.

Second Meadow, upstream from the campground. Angler—Craig Mathews.

3
Slough Creek

As Howard Back remarked in his splendid *The Waters of Yellowstone with Rod and Fly* (Dodd, Mead and Co., 1938), this stream is locally pronounced "Sloo." It is a cutthroat stream of rare beauty with an abundance of splendid fish, and a good insect population. It rises in the Beartooth Range, not far from the famous Grasshopper Glacier, where grasshoppers a thousand years dead can still be seen in the glacier's frozen face.

A little over sixteen miles of the stream runs through the Park, from the high mountains just west of Cooke City down into the Lamar Valley. It is tributary to the Lamar, which itself is tributary to the Yellowstone. About 70 percent of the stream runs through open meadows; the remainder is cascades and riffles running through rocky timber stretches and steep canyons.

Anglers regard the river as being in four sections. The first mile above its juncture with the Lamar is a cascade-riffle stretch through a steep canyon. It is not much fished. The reason is that from the bench at the head of this canyon to the second canyon, a half-mile above Slough Creek Campground, are three miles of really excellent water much more easily reached. It is pools, runs and riffles, one after the other, through an open, meadow-laced basin, and the largest fish in the creek are to be found here. But they are *very* difficult to catch in the larger sizes (twenty inches and up). Don't ever believe that these cutthroat are as simple to fool as their more numerous kin of the Yellowstone. These big bruisers in the open meadow pools are as tough to deceive as a five-pound brown.

Unlike many Yellowstone Park streams, this one is not paralleled by roadways. It is approachable by automobile only at the head of the first canyon, at the trailhead and at the campground.

The trailhead marks the start of the trail that leads to the meadows above the second canyon. First Meadow is about a forty-five-minute walk, Second Meadow is a three-hour walk if you are in good condition.

The lower section contains the larger fish, although they are not so numerous. The insect structure is much more varied in the section downstream from the campground than that in the meadows above. This, and the possibility of a portion of the fish being rainbow-cutthroat hybrids, are reasons biologists give for this stretch being more difficult to fish with success.

Conversely, the fish in the meadows above second canyon are far more readily caught. The catch rate in First Meadow is about five fish per hour and the fish will average fifteen inches. This area is second only to the Yellowstone above Hayden Valley in terms of angler success.

The stretch from the canyon beyond the Lamar to the campground is about three miles of really excellent water. Lying in the lap of the basin, it is an area of surpassing beauty. To the south, across the valley of the Lamar, which Osborne Russell in *Journal of a Trapper (1834–1843)* calls Paradise Valley, one sees the rolling slopes and immense dome of Mount Washburn. To the north looms the great bulk of the Beartooth Range including Granite Peak, the highest mountain in Montana. Eastward lie the sculptured peaks of the Absarokas, and to the west the Black Canyon of the Yellowstone is a winding slash in the landscape. There is beauty of every kind to soothe and calm and put one at peace.

But there are distractions also, in the numbers of animals and birds that vie for one's attention. When Dan Callaghan and I came to this spot in the fall of 1982 to get pictures for this book, we were constantly—and happily—distracted. An enormous herd of buffalo grazed in the open area between the Lamar and VIP Pool on Slough Creek. Antelope frisked around the buffalo herd. Two mule deer does and their fawns browsed peacefully beside the road. Hawks, falcons, eagles and ospreys, grounded by a low ceiling and intermittent drizzle, perched on trees and rocks and the scarps of cliffs. Geese sailed majestically over the surface of little lakes, and mallards paddled and gabbled happily in the sloughs that give the creek its name. It was hard to keep our minds on our work.

We were further distracted by a hatch of huge gray mayflies coming off the dimpled surface of VIP Pool. I had to laugh at Dan, who is as devout a photographer as I am a fly-fisher, crouching, kneeling, sitting in the 50-degree water in his Levis, to get photographs of the emerging naturals. Later we stood entranced to watch a large trout feeding on the emerging mayflies alongside a boulder in the faster water below the tail of the pool.

When one comes to the stream at the old ford that divides VIP Pool, there is so much of this kind of water in sight that one may be fooled into believing that the entire

VIP Pool.

First Meadow, upstream from the campground.

stretch up to the pool above the campground is like this. It is not. Just around the corner above the upper reaches of VIP Pool, one comes to the first of many riffles. These are quite the nicest riffles for the fly-fisher that one will find anywhere. Most are out in the open with nothing to interfere with the back cast. The stream is just wide enough to be handled with an easy cast, the current is mostly obliging, seldom contrary. It is one of fly-fishing's greatest joys to drift a high-riding dry fly down such a bouncing riffle and watch it disappear in the shattering rise of a slashing trout. The trout here strike any floating fly vigorously, and in July, August and September they will hit hopper patterns with a smash that sends spray flying into the meadow grass.

If they are not coming to the dry fly, they will often hit a big, black stone fly nymph pattern with equal vigor. But if you fish the smaller mayfly and caddis nymphal patterns, or the soft hackled wets that simulate the caddis pupa, you must be ever so alert, for the wily rascals take these with an almost imperceptible sucking sip which often will go entirely unnoticed unless you're on the *qui vive*.

So, one fishes his merry way up this lovely stream. It is much more than a day's fishing to cover this stretch unless you are the flail-and-run type of angler. If you are, you'll not only miss the beauty but the greatest pleasures of this stretch, which should be taken in easy sips, not swallowed at a gulp.

To reach First Meadow, one starts at the trailhead about halfway between the highway and the campground. Use this trail, because trying to go up the canyon from the campground to First Meadow is for mountain climbers in good condition. It is marked, and the sign gives the distance to various spots in miles. But we fishers prefer to think of them in times, and by this measure it's about an easy forty-five-minute walk to First Meadow. The initial few minutes are up a very steep slope, so start off easy. Also, you won't need to wade in First Meadow, so wear your hiking boots.

Take a net. No matter what your inclination is, fish are more easily and more humanely handled in a net. A number of studies, including one by the U.S. Fish and Wildlife Service in Yellowstone Park, document that fish that are netted survive at a much higher rate than fish taken into one's hands—provided that the fly is removed from the fish while in the net, and the fish is returned to the water without being otherwise handled. Also, one can bring a fish to net without fighting it to exhaustion that would be dangerous to its life. Many waters in the area covered herein are catch-and-release *only*. There is no point in releasing a dead fish.

First Meadow is actually a subalpine basin, ringed with forested slopes and high mountains. The stream is winding, as are most basin meadow streams. Near to where the trail comes in, off to the left and back downstream a bit, is an enormous pool with gigantic boulders. There are some very fine fish here, but they are fish that require some catching. By all means have a go at them if it pleases you, but if you wish to reach the five-fish-per-hour average here, you'll do better in the regular run of stream.

They are beautiful fish, these Slough Creek cutthroats, butter yellow with golden olive backs and black-spotted sides, purple cheek plates and the typical orange slashes under the jaw. They are a prime sporting fish as well, so treat them with respect, and release them alive so that you or another may come to catch them again.

Most times they will come willingly to a well-presented dry fly, and in July, August and up to mid-September a hopper pattern will produce action of the showiest kind. The bottom here, for the most part, is sand silt or very fine gravel. The stream-bred naturals are mostly small. The exceptions are dragon and damsel flies, and a nymph representing them is the best bet when fish are not coming to the dry fly. If neither dry fly, hopper or dragon-damsel nymph produces, the soft-hackle wets are a good bet.

Beyond First Meadow, up the climbing trail, now next to the stream, now not, it is a little more than two hours to Second Meadow. Here the stream is smaller but more difficult to fish. This area is perhaps the greatest favorite in the Park for the young, hike-in-and-stay-overnight anglers, and they compose nearly all who fish here. Like many young people today, they have a deep respect for the environment and for the creatures in it. I always wish them well in Second Meadow, but I no longer join them there.

When fishing anywhere along lovely Slough Creek, lift your eyes from the water on occasion and look around. You are in the most beautiful part of the largest angler's paradise in the world. Take time to enjoy it. Though under the kind of protection it enjoys, it will be here forever, you will not. Look up, and you will have scenes and memories to last a lifetime.

NATURALS AND ARTIFICIALS

The most successful fly for most of the season is a hopper pattern. Have a good selection in sizes and colors and you will not often be skunked. Dave's Hopper, Gartside's Pheasant Hopper, Joe's Hopper—all are good, and for reasons not known to me, one will work at times when another will not. Sizes 6 and 8 are best.

Fishing the nymph, one will need damsel and dragon fly nymphs in the meadows, because these carnivorous brutes are always found in smooth bottoms where other aquatic insects are. Good patterns are Kaufmann's Lake Dragon in brown, Beaverpelt, Bailey's Damsel and various marabou damsel patterns. I use my own Assam Dragon in Light and Dark (tan and brown) and my Fair Damsel and Green Damsel patterns. These are only available as commercial patterns in The Trout Shop or perhaps Bob Jacklin's Fly Shop, both in West Yellowstone. Size 4 in dragon and 6 in damsel nymphs are needed.

For the mayflies, general mayfly types are better than exact patterns. The Gray Nymph, Martinez Black and Zug Bug in sizes 10, 12 and 14 will suffice most times.

Caddis are more numerous than other types, in this as well as most area streams. Here one will find *Brachycentrus* and *Rhyacophila*, in several species, as well as *Helicopsyche*, *Chimarra* and perhaps others. However, the fish are not unduly selective to these underwater forms. One needs a good selection of grouse- and partridge-hackled wets; Grouse and Green, Partridge and Orange, Grouse and Yellow and Grouse and Grey in 12, 14 and 16, plus perhaps the best general wet fly ever invented, the Gold Ribbed Hare's Ear in the same sizes. I'd want the Hare's Ears weighted.

For dries, Blue Dun in 16 and 18 will take care of the *Baetis* hatches although in fall a Blue Winged Olive in the same sizes is better. For an occasional unidentified ginger hatch one should have Light Cahill or Grey Fox Variant in 12 and 14.

The more numerous caddis are obliging by coming off mostly in shades of gray or brown. So Colorado King and Elk Hair Caddis in those shades and in sizes 12, 14, 16 and 18 will fill the bill most times.

When no hatch or hoppers are about, we in this country favor the Royal Wulff, Hair Wing Variant (House and Lot) Goofus Bug and Renegade in sizes 10 and 12. The purpose of using these is the same as for using a club to hit a mule between the eyes. You want to gain the attention of the trout at once—and smaller, less showy flies often won't.

One fly you don't hear much about anymore but which is perhaps the best all-round dry fly going, is the Adams. I'd have it in sizes 10, 12, 14, 16, 18 and maybe even 20. It's often saved me from getting skunked. Try it, you'll like it. I've not yet identified the large dark gray mayfly that Dan and I observed in September 1982.

Lamar Valley.

4
Lamar River

When Osborne Russell first saw the valley of the Lamar in the mid-1830s, he called it Paradise Valley and wished he could spend the rest of his life there. Today there are tourists and fishermen who spend their entire vacations in this lovely, peaceful place.

The Lamar begins in the Absarokas, in Hoodoo Basin on the south side of Hoodoo Peak and the east edge of the Park. It runs for a full thirty miles northwest down a crooked, curving canyon before it comes into sight along the Tower Junction—Cooke City road and is joined by Soda Butte Creek coming down from the north. Here begins the Lamar Valley and the fishable portion of the river. In about thirty miles of river run, the Lamar has dropped almost 3,000 feet, or 100 feet per mile. This abrupt fall and strong flow make it not too hospitable for larger fish as well as making it hard work to get to. For that reason it is little fished above the Junction Pool.

The precipitous flow above causes problems for the river here and farther down. The headwaters region among the towering peaks of the Absarokas is an area of violent summer thunderstorms. The water rages off the bare granite peaks that reach above the timberline, pours over the fragile soil, cuts down the curving canyon and brings a torrent of mud to its union with the Soda Butte. One can stand at the Junction Pool just hours after such a storm and see the two streams come together, the Soda Butte clear as gin, the Lamar the color of pea soup. The line of demarcation will continue for a half-mile or so more, one-half of the river gin clear, the other pea soup. Farther along, the entire river will be thick with mud and fishing will become very poor for perhaps a day.

But the clearing of the stream puts the fish on the feed. For the one who is there at this time, the fishing can be fabulous. These summer storms are capricious, however,

Upstream from the confluence with Soda Butte Creek. Absarokas is in the background.

and one cannot know when they will come. This is one reason that many visitors like to camp as near as possible to the Lamar Valley.

The Lamar is otherwise a friendly, gentle stream of runs and riffles and an occasional meadow pool. Except for the canyon section where it cuts down rather swiftly to join the Yellowstone, it is much alike from Junction Pool to the head of the canyon.

For reasons not yet explained, the cutthroat migrate or rove about, upstream and down. This will cause puzzlement among anglers; the riffle or run that produced well this week may appear as barren as a snowbank next week. The answer, for the angler, is to move up or down and try to locate where the fish are holding at this time.

Once the fish are located, they are not difficult to lure, though they are unduly wary. They will, most times, come to a high-riding dry fly or a colorful wet if it is presented with some care. The currents during normal flow are not unduly contrary although the wind occasionally is.

There are about twelve miles of river from the confluence with the Soda Butte to the Yellowstone. About half is in meadow valley, about half is canyon-type water. The two stretches must be approached and fished differently.

The river is what the British call a "spate stream," a gentler term for a river that fluctuates greatly in volume due to flooding. Between spates, the river may cover only about half the bottom that it does in full flow. This causes a change in holding areas and may explain why the fish move about. They are not accustomed to "permanent" holds as in streams of more stable flow.

There is a slight benching effect here and there through the valley section. At certain seasons the flatter areas overflow and are marshy; some of these marshes are semipermanent. One must use care crossing from the highway parking turnouts, to the river, lest you find yourself cut off from the stream. One such marsh is just across from the Lamar ranger station, but this is also one of the better fishing stretches. The river is mostly close to the road, but about a mile before it first enters the canyon, it swings away a half-mile or so, and then returns to near the road at the canyon head. As it wanders through the valley, its curves create deeper spots and this, generally, is where the fish are. Seldom will you find them in the riffles, and only rarely in the deeper short runs between corner pools.

I have found it best to proceed upstream, whether fishing wet or dry. Also, where there is little cover, staying back or crouching, even kneeling if you can manage it, is a help. There are not many places for the trout to hide, nor many truly deep holes where the fish feel safe. In this respect, the meadow sections of the Lamar are like many spate streams in other parts of the country.

The canyon stretch is totally different water. It is varied, with pocket water, fast runs, deep riffles, chutes that approach cascades and some little flat water, which still has a good current flow. There are huge basketball–to–sofa–sized boulders just about everywhere. It is difficult to enter in some places, fairly easily reached in others.

I like this kind of water. It offers a variety of challenges, it has larger insects (the

Near Ranger Station (above). Lamar Valley near Ranger Station (below).

Near picnic ground (above). Cutthroat Trout on the Lamar River (below).

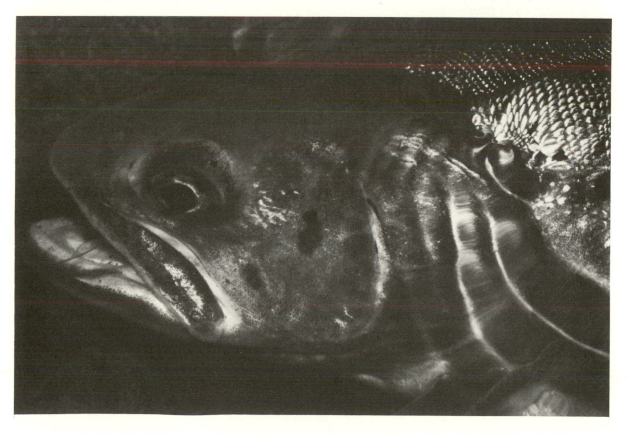

giant stone fly nymph, *Pteronarcys*) and its fish seem more opportunistic. This, plus the quick strike on wet or dry fly made necessary by current speed and rapid shifts of direction, make it more exciting for me. Also, there seems to be more frequent hatches of more numerous insects.

I like to fish large high-riding dry flies in such water. Trout in this kind of water seem to want a fly large enough to be easily seen and worth the effort to come up from their deep boulder lies. I was first exposed to this theory in 1946 while serving as a ranger in Yosemite National Park. The section of the Merced near Arch Rock is much like the Lamar in the canyon and a visiting angler using a Fan Wing Royal Coachman was by far the most successful angler I encountered on my daily creel checks. I've since found the practice successful in such rocky fast water over most of the West and Alaska. Besides, it is easier than trying to keep a smaller imitative fly afloat in these churning runs and, of course, these large showy flies are more easily seen and kept track of.

The big black stone fly nymph is a must in such waters in our area, and a good caddis larval imitation also. I favor my Skunk Hair Caddis pattern in such places, and I believe that The Trout Shop (Bud Lilly's former shop) in West Yellowstone may be the only place in the entire country that carries this pattern commercially. The Gold Ribbed Hare's Ear in large (number 8) size is also effective. The Black Woolly Worm is largely used by local anglers.

The more agile and adventurous angler will find the section of the Lamar from the confluence of Slough Creek down to where it joins the Yellowstone to be excellent water for larger than average fish. It is also water where one will find more than average dunkings. It is not much fished because of the difficulties of getting in and out and also while there. But it has appeal of a special kind for one who likes isolated, difficult waters not far from a good road.

New regulations have done much to improve the Lamar as a quality fishery. Because of its spate nature, it has shown irregularity in angler success, but over the past few years has improved in both size and numbers of trout. An interim report issued by the U.S. Fish and Wildlife Service which manages Park streams (through the Park Administration) indicated an average size of seventeen inches for cutthroat caught by anglers in 1980, but this was later revised downward to fifteen inches, which I believe to be nearer the actual figure. But angler satisfaction is generally higher on the Lamar than other Park streams. This doesn't mean that anglers catch more or larger fish, but that they are happier with the fishing and all that goes with it. Anglers tend to become much attached to this river and its beautiful, peaceful surroundings.

NATURALS AND ARTIFICIALS

The bottom of the Lamar has areas of silt or sand silt caused by the frequent flooding. Insects in such bottoms are nearly always small *except* for dragon and damsel nymphs, which are always found in such bottom types that hold other insects. So, have the nymphs of these two in brown and tan in sizes 6 and 8.

The only small mayfly I've been able to identify here is *Centroptilum* species, the Golden Olive Spinner, size 20. It emerges usually in October, *but* emergence times will vary on any spate stream. In gravel bottoms one will find *Epeorus* species, the Western Quill Gordon, size 12. The Adams in that size will suffice most times if you don't have the Quill, and a Blue Dun may also work.

There are scattered hatches of *Callibaetis*, *Drunella grandis*, *Ephemerella coloradensis* and *Heptagenia* along the Lamar. Only rarely are these prolific enough to produce a strong feeding rise. But one should have Pale Morning Dun 16, Blue Winged Olive 14, Adams 14 and a Light Cahill 14, just to be prepared. For nymphs, the Hendrickson 14, Zug Bug 12 and 14 and the Hare's Ear 12 and 14 will cover most mayfly types in the meadows.

The rocky stretches, particularly in the canyon, will hold at least three species of stone fly. *Pteronarcys californica* will be largest and most plentiful. The Black Woolly Worm or one of the many local nymphal imitations will be most useful in sizes 4, 3 or 4XL. For *Hesperoperla pacifica* and *Doroneuria theodora* (both formerly *Acroneuria* genus) one needs an Amber or Golden Stone nymph in sizes 6, 3XL or 8, 3XL.

In June or early July, one *may* hit the emergence of *Pteronarcys* (salmonfly) in the canyon, especially near the Yellowstone, and one can have a ball with the Sofa Pillow, Bird's Stonefly or Parks' Stonefly (by Richard Parks of Parks' Fly Shop, Gardiner) in sizes 6 and 4, 3XL. As late as mid-August one will encounter the yellow stone flies (*Hesperoperla* and *Doroneuria*) in the canyon or even upstream. A yellow-bodied Bucktail Caddis, or a yellow-bodied Joe's Hopper, size 6 or 8, will fill the need for these.

The most prevalent caddis—the most numerous insect in all trout streams in this area—are *Brachycentrus*, *Rhyacophila* and *Hydropsyche*. There are others, but again *most* adult caddis are gray or brown, and the Elk Hair Caddis and Colorado King in sizes 12, 14, 16 and 18 are always needed, in shades of gray and in brown. Some with green bodies are helpful if the fish are being difficult.

In the soft-hackle wets one needs grouse hackle with gray, tan or green bodies. A primrose yellow body is very good *if* you can find it in the shops.

The Elk Hair Caddis and Colorado King are almost exactly alike in design, *but* one may have to obtain both patterns to get the correct sizes in both colors—gray and brown. These are the number one fly in sales in area fly shops but any suitable dry caddis pattern in the correct sizes and colors may be used with good success.

Lewis River Canyon.

5
Lewis River

Shoshone Lake lies in the southern-facing open end of a hairpin-shaped fold of the continental divide in south central Yellowstone Park. It is formed by the input of De Lacy, Shoshone, Moose and Cold Mountain creeks. The Lewis River runs full blown out of its southeast arm at 7,790 feet above sea level.

The Lewis is really three rivers in one. Its three sections are separated by a lake (Lewis Lake) and a waterfall, and these create three rivers that are completely different from each other, not only in appearance, but sometimes in the fish they hold, and certainly in the methods used to fish them.

Though most of us regard the Lewis as having three distinct sections with three differing personalities, there are actually four such sections. But the section in the deep, steep, rough, dangerous Lewis Canyon does not hold fish worth either the labor or the risk of going after them. I did once, when I was young, strong as an ox and just as smart. But never again. So, we will herein disregard that section of the river.

The section from the falls to the head of the canyon is regarded as a broad, many-channeled meadow stream. It is now, and has always been (at least since 1948, when I first fished it) the most puzzling and exasperating trout stream in the country. And it is not only anglers that it has puzzled. For at least nine years biologists have been baffled by its inconsistencies and contradictions—so much so, that in 1976 they designated it a special no-kill study area. The river is cold, it has good oxygen content, abundant fish food, plenty of depth and cover—in fact, most everything a fish could want. And it has trout. But they are usually under eight inches, or over eighteen. There seems to be no middle class at all. And that's strange.

Lewis River Falls.

At the top of Lewis River Channel between Lewis and Shoshone Lakes. Shoshone Lake is in the background.

Much of the bottom is covered by silt, caused by the beaver and muskrats working in the marshy meadows around some of the channels and tributary streams. The insects, except for dragon-damsel species, are small. There is a scattering of small- to medium-size mayflies, and, as usual, many species of caddis.

The river here exhibits different faces. Some of the broad, sloping-bottomed stretches are relatively featureless and hold few fish, although some very large ones will be seen if one moves carefully. I get the feeling that these big trout are cruisers. The many channels are varied in size and sometimes in appearance. Mostly they are winding, fairly deep, with undercut banks, pothole bottoms and fairly slow currents. Typical dry fly tactics work most times, but occasionally fail. Then a big high floater is needed to stir up the fish. Hopper season is good some years, not good others. I have a feeling that the marshes have something to do with this. When the marshes are dry and somewhat firm, there are more hoppers. When the marshes remain wet and spongy all summer, there are fewer. This may not always hold true; I only fish this section once or twice a year, and it's difficult to pinpoint things without being more familiar with this baffling piece of water.

In general, I'd recommend using regular dry fly tactics or fishing the big dragon-damsel nymphs. Some friends do well now and then with streamers and leeches, but just as often, they are skunked. The only things that make this section appealing are its broad meadow beauty, its proximity to the road and the very occasional large trout one succeeds in deceiving. Then, it's only a ten-minute drive and a ten-minute walk to the section above the falls. This has some of the same inconsistencies of the lower section—but they're a bit more solvable.

One can approach the above-the-falls section by a short, steep climb to the head of the falls, or from the south end of Lewis Lake Campground. Drive as far south down into the campground as near the lakeshore as possible and find a parking spot. Hike up over the low ridge between campground and lake (about one hundred yards), turn left along the beach and proceed to the outlet. The whole walk is less than a half-mile, over the low ridge and along the lake. Take some advice from one who has been there: *Do not* try to reach the river any other way, such as through the woods south of the campground. This is the most terrible piece of down timber, rock–and–boulder–strewn terrain I have ever seen. During the 1860s a group of gold seekers made their way through this area, and one of them called it "jackstraw hell." They were on horseback and some days a full day's travel would net them but a mile and a half.

This stream in this stretch has the appearance of some eastern hardwood forest streams. It is a constant succession of pools and riffles, with an occasional cascade with a plunge pool eddy. It is picture-book pretty.

The resident trout are mostly small. But big browns run *down* the stream from the Lewis Lake outlet in the fall, and some remain in choice locations they have found. There is a puzzling thing that also happens in the fall. The lake is full of lake trout, some to forty pounds, and some autumns this stretch (familiarly called the Lewis outlet) will

Lewis River Falls (above). Mackinaw Trout under water between Lewis Lake and Shoshone Lake (below).

Between Lewis Lake and Shoshone Lake.

be loaded with eighteen- to twenty-two-inch lake trout as well as big browns. I sent a young Canadian friend over there a few falls ago and he caught twenty-three trout over sixteen inches, almost evenly divided between browns and lakers. Nobody seems to know what the lake trout are doing there, but they are there most falls, and in numbers. They are a happy surprise on the end of your line when you're expecting a big brown.

During the rest of the year, this portion of the stream is like prospecting for gold—the larger fish are where you find them. It is a very pleasant stream to fish, with its friendly riffles and pleasant pools. The mayflies here are sparse in numbers and mostly small. Caddis are by far the dominant insect and many are the net spinners—*Hydropsyche*, *Chimarra* and perhaps others. Some are varieties that build no cases until they pupate, and the different genera emerge at different times all summer and fall. For this stream one wants a good supply of soft-hackle wets, the Hare's Ear in several sizes and the good caddis dries in brown or gray.

The fishing is spotty. Some riffles and pools appear to hold no trout, while others almost identical in appearance will yield several fish. For most areas, one needs only a floating line to fish either dry or wet. For some reason, the big *Pteronarcys* stone fly nymph imitations are not as useful here as in most other streams where they are found. The cold water *does* limit their numbers.

The regular season fishing is standard in tactics and techniques. Match the hatch when there is one, fish big showy dries or soft-hackle wets when no flies are showing. Hoppers in season and some ant imitations are helpful.

In the fall, it is a different ball game. The running spawners are not usually regular feeders, they seem to hit more out of irritation than hunger. Big streamers, leeches, deerhair mice and huge floaters seem to be the best choice, but often it's trial and error until you find the taking fly and method.

In October (Park fishing ends October 31) and sometimes in late September one will find the quarter-mile of stream below the outlet to be jammed with large browns and lakers. If one finds the taking lure for the day, it's possible to catch and release forty or more of these active big trout.

Across Lewis Lake is the four-mile-long, rocky, pocket water stretch of the upper Lewis River. This section, the river's headwaters, is locally known as "the Channel." In summer it seems to be an all-or-nothing piece of water. You get skunked or you knock 'em dead. There seems to be no in between.

It is reached by powerboat across Lewis Lake or by trail from the Thumb–South Entrance road. If you take the powerboat route, you can tow a canoe and paddle upstream from the river's mouth, fishing as you go (powerboats are not allowed in the river). Or you can anchor on the north shore of the river's mouth where it enters the lake and take the trail upstream. This trail is about a mile shorter than the one coming in from the road, but it is not as good a trail and there are far more ups and downs.

The resident fish move about in this stretch. One must seek them out in summer. Standard wet and dry fly tactics apply up to about mid-September. In fall, up to season closing, one fishes for the running spawners with the same flies and methods as used in the Lewis Lake outlet mentioned earlier.

This stretch, like the other two sections covered, has its peculiarities. More fish appear to run *down* the Channel from Shoshone Lake than run up from Lewis Lake. Biologists are unable to find any reason for this. But it is a regular fall occurrence and one's chances are far better in the first quarter-mile below Shoshone Lake than in the rest of the stream. I've seen the browns packed in this stretch by the hundreds.

Of course, fall weather in this area is often less than ideal. Fall winds can come up suddenly and can be deadly. We've had several people caught on Shoshone Lake in small craft which capsized and the people perished in the cold water. The odds are very good in the fall that one will encounter wind or snow, but the size of the fish and their numbers make it worth the gamble. Many good fly-fishermen I know love this stretch of river above all others in the fall.

NATURALS AND ARTIFICIALS

The naturals in this river are somewhat different in each of its sections, and do not reach the numbers they do in most other streams of the area. *Pteronarcys californica*, the giant stone fly, is random and sparse. Smaller stone flies, *Arcynopteryx* and the rare slow-water form, *Nemoura*, are found in slower stretches with smooth bottoms. The caddis are the most numerous of insect types: One will find *Rhyacophila*, *Brachycentrus* and some *Limnephilis* in the streams and even along the wind-lapped shores of the two lakes.

Mayflies are scarce and of the smaller species; *Ephemerella*, *Baetis* and *Epeorus* are most common but not plentiful in the streams. The lakes will have occasional good hatches that make it worthwhile to fish the dry fly at such times.

The artificials one needs in summer are gray and brown Colorado King or Elk Hair Caddis dries, sizes 14 through 18; the soft-hackle wets with gray, green, yellow and orange bodies, size 12; some Hare's Ears, hopper patterns, a few Black and Red Ant dry patterns and some of the big showy dries—Royal Wulff, Goofus Bug, Hair Wing Variant or Renegade—in 8 and 10.

Match-the-hatch mayfly types are sort of like parachutes—you seldom need them but when you do, nothing else will do the job. So, have Quill Gordon or Hendrickson in 12 and 14, Adams in the same sizes, Pale Morning Dun in 16 and Blue Winged Olive also in 16.

In the fall, big streamers; Spruce, Brown or Green Marabou Muddlers; a sculpin pattern, and a leech, all in sizes 2 to 2/0 are the most taking. Also, at times, a Deerhair Mouse or a huge all-hackle dry—Brown or Grey Bivisible in size 6 or 8—will result in action that is startling in its suddenness and explosive nature. Using these latter dry flies one will find that the old George La Branche trick of "artificial hatch"—repeated floats through the same area—is the best way to obtain results.

Elk and calf at the second bridge.

6

Firehole River

The Firehole rises in tiny Madison Lake which lies in a marshy subalpine basin at 8,200 feet along a north-facing slope of the continental divide. From the lake to the bridge on the Old Faithful–Thumb road under which it passes, this is a tiny, cold, winding brook trout stream that also holds a few pan-size browns.

Below the Old Faithful water supply intake, down to the bridge above Biscuit Basin and the mouth of the Little Firehole, is a two- or three-mile stretch that is currently closed to fishing. It never was really good fishing water, except for small spot locations, such as just behind Old Faithful and near Morning Glory Pool. Its closure, to protect the many thermal features, is a very small loss for the fisherman.

The Little Firehole is joined just above its junction with the main river by Iron Spring Creek, locally called Iron Creek. These two streams are much cooler than the Firehole itself and are run-up streams for large trout in July and August of warm years. If summer remains cool, with considerable rain and snow (a not unusual condition at this 7,500 foot level), the larger trout will remain in the big river with its better, more secure holds and more plentiful insects.

But if the summer has been warm and very dry, big trout will run up these cooler streams. There will be some very good fish just above the footbridge across the Little Firehole–Iron Creek stem, and just below the junction of the two streams. There will be some few fish in the Little Firehole above the confluence of the two streams, but in general this stream is *too* cold for comfort for the warm water–loving trout of the main stream.

Iron Creek will run some 6 to 10 degrees cooler than the main stream. It is somewhat larger than the Little Firehole and is much more favored by big run-up browns and rainbows. To put things in perspective, when the temperature of the main river reaches 80 degrees Fahrenheit, the larger trout, with their smaller temperature change tolerance, will commence to move into the two cooler streams. These trout are accustomed to temperatures of 70 to 78 degrees in summer and, in fact, prefer a temperature of 70 to 75, because for eighty generations, that has been the normal midsummer daytime temperature of the Firehole.

In the early 1970s a series of earthquakes more severe than normal took place near the Firehole headwaters. This region suffers about 200 quakes a year of up to 4.5 on the Richter Scale, but some of the quakes in the early 1970s reached 6.5 on the Richter. Apparently this opened up new or greater high temperature flows into the river, raising the daytime high temperatures to the high 80s by 1979. In the mid-seventies this caused great numbers of large trout to leave the Firehole and enter Iron Creek during the hottest part of summer. These high temperatures also caused the growth and reproductive rates of the trout to drop dramatically, reducing both the size and numbers of trout in the stream.

This phenomenon has caused a controversy between the fishermen and the biologists of the U.S. Fish and Wildlife Service who manage the fisheries resources in Yellowstone Park. These biologists maintain no such temperature change has taken place. When we fishermen who have taken temps in the Firehole over the years (I've been doing it since 1948) tell them of our measurements, they dismiss them as unreliable. When I was told this by the assistant to the chief biologist in 1979, I asked what the U.S. Fish and Wildlife Service records showed. There were no records, he said, we've never taken temperatures on the Firehole. When I then asked how he could say that no temperature change had taken place, he replied loftily, "We know." When I said this did not seem to be at all scientific, he stalked off in a rage. That's where the matter stands now. And although scientists in two other disciplines, those of microbiology and waterfowl, have confirmed the rise in temperature, the USFWS refuses to change its opinion.

I have covered this in some detail because at one time the Firehole, in my opinion, was the finest dry fly stream in the nation. The fish were superwary and elusive, but a skillfull dry fly fisher in the years 1950 to 1970 could expect to take ten to twenty trout in a day, averaging over two pounds each with several of three or more pounds. That is no longer the case, and each year scores of fly-fishermen come to me and say: "Charlie, what's wrong? What's happened to the Firehole?"

I may be wrong about how the temperature change came about, but I am not wrong about the fact that it has taken place, nor about its effects on the quality of the fishery. Today, the average trout one catches are twelve inches or under and there are not so many of them. There are still occasional lunkers taken—in 1982 one of over five pounds came out of Muleshoe Bend. But these can only exist near a cold water input that also gives them security in the form of depth or cover, and there are a very limited number of such spots.

Upper Goose Lake Meadows.

However, there appears to be a change taking place again in the river; temperatures in the stream during 1980, 1981 and 1982 did not top 80 degrees. These have been unusually cool summers with more than normal amounts of rain and snow. Whether it was this condition that kept the river cooler, or whether more tremors have reversed things in the underground plumbing, bringing more cooler water to the surface, only time will tell. By most standards the Firehole is still a fine stream, it is one of the most beautiful and its ease of approach is unparalleled. For those reasons it is still much favored by those willing to come to terms with its diminished quality as a trout fishery.

Biscuit Basin is still one of the best dry fly stretches, and though the fish are smaller, they are no less difficult, and this is a very challenging piece of water. With conditions as they have been for the past three years, one can now and then find a nice pod of larger fish in the main river just above and below where the Iron Creek–Little Firehole stem enters. These are pre–run-up fish holding here in the cooler flow, waiting for a change which will either force them into the smaller, cooler streams, or allow them to return to their normal holds and lies in the Firehole itself.

Biscuit Basin itself is about a mile of winding meadow stream, deep in places, with an abundance of bottom drop-offs, weed beds and undercut banks providing holds and lies for the trout. The trout of this stretch are almost half-and-half rainbows and browns. It has always been too warm for brookies, which are mostly found now in the cooler water above Keppler Cascades. When the river was first stocked with trout in 1889 (it was barren of fish above Firehole Falls when white men first saw it in the 1830s) brook trout from the East were put into the stream. These quickly fled upstream to cooler water above Old Faithful. In 1890 browns were stocked, and in 1897 a woman named Mary Trowbridge Townsend wrote a lovely piece in *Outing Magazine* in which she tells of catching a "gloriously colored Von Behr (brown) trout of four pounds."

The river was allegedly named by Jim Bridger in 1851 when he was showing a group of mountain men from the southern Rockies through the Park. It is said that Bridger told them that the river was heated by friction from running over its bedrock bottom, but this sophisticated observation does not fit what is known about the uneducated mountain man.

This bedrock bottom is evident in the Firehole throughout its length. Boulders broken off the cliffs of Firehole Canyon and strewn along the river bottom make it appear different than the rest of the stream, but if you are interested enough to move some of these boulders, you will find them resting on bedrock.

To return to Biscuit Basin, sophisticated dry fly and emergent nymphs methods are used here. While an unusually long leader is not required, I've found that a much longer than usual tippet is, because the currents are much more contrary than one thinks.

In 1948, when I first fished Biscuit Basin, I had come up through Jackson's Hole. I had stopped at Bob Carmichael's Fly Shop in Moose to ask him about fishing the Snake River in the Hole. When Bob found that I was on my way to fish the Firehole, he told me that in order to catch fish there I'd have to have some of his Edward Hewitt patent

Middle of Biscuit Basin.

Near the second bridge. Angler—Ernie Schwiebert.

nitrate-stained black leaders in 5X. So I bought a few 5X leader tippets, which I promptly lost somewhere in my duffle. But Bob had convinced me that my leaders for the Firehole had to be black, and when the fish kept refusing my size 16 to 22 dry flies, I was convinced that it was because I didn't have black leader tippets.

The only black material I had with me was a spool of size A black fly tying thread. I put eighteen inches of this on the end of my leader and lo!, started catching fish. When I came up again in 1949, I'd forgotten the black thread. My first few days were fishless. I madly searched my duffle for black thread but could only find some size A red that I'd used for steelhead flies. In desperation, I put eighteen inches of that on my leader tip. And, what do you know, I caught fish just as well as I had with black thread. Later on I experimented with other colors and found that color was of no importance—nor was diameter. The only thing that counted was flexibility, and I now obtain that by using a four- or five-foot tippet of 5X or 6X.

Fishing the smooth stretches of the Firehole, dry or wet, still requires such subtlety. Biscuit Basin, Muleshoe Bend, Goose Lake Meadows, Ojo Caliente Bend, the Broads—all these pieces of difficult water require every skill one can muster because these are wild fish that have been fished over for ninety years, and they have learned much in that time.

Coming down from the lower end of Biscuit Basin Meadows, one encounters two miles of riffle and shallow pool water. This is a less fishworthy stretch than the water either above or below. At the lower end one comes to a high bank on the left, formed of siliceous sinter, the whitish-gray material found around geysers and other thermal features. Beginning at the downstream end of this is a quarter-mile stretch of broken-bottomed pools and runs that is quite good and seldom fished, though it is less than a hundred yards from the road. Then comes a half-mile more of shallow riffles and another high bank of sinter, again on the left. This used to be an excellent stretch, with some large trout lying in the channel next to the bank. Ray Bergman wrote extensively about it in the thirties, when three-pounders could regularly be found here. But it has silted in with geyser debris over the years and the larger fish are no longer there.

Just beyond the lower end of this bank is an abrupt break in the bedrock bottom and a short cascade and plunge pool. The stretch from there to the Upper Iron Bridge, about three-eighths of a mile, is quite good, excellent with dry fly or emergent nymph as needed. Below the bridge a long riffle and run reaches to the upper end of Muleshoe Bend. Before the late warming of the river there were big stone fly nymphs of *Pteronarcys* and *Acroneuria* (now *Calineuria*) here, and at the foot of the faster stretches, in deeper water, an occasional large trout could be found waiting for the drifting nymph. This is no longer true, although smaller fish can be taken with some regularity.

The tight loop of Muleshoe Bend is still a half-mile of excellent dry fly water with some good fish in it, as well as many smaller ones. One parks at the road turnout at the apex of the bend on the high bank there and watches for the hatch to commence. I've not found it too profitable to fish this stretch if no flies were showing.

Above the second bridge. Angler—Jack Hemingway.

Near the second bridge.

Muleshoe Bend.

Upper Goose Lake Meadows.

There is a long riffle from the lower end of Muleshoe through the rest of Midway Geyser Basin. It is right beside the road and is an excellent piece of water for the beginner or children. It is loaded with insect life, mostly small, and the rough but not too uneven bottom offers good footing.

Below Excelsior Spring, which pours a steaming cataract of 200 degree water into the river, there is a long, shallow stretch of relatively fishless water leading into the head of Goose Lake Meadows, a long piece of mostly gliding dry fly water. By dry fly water, I do not mean that other methods cannot be used with success, but that the appearance and conditions truly bespeak the dry fly. From mid-July till late September this is a grasshopper stretch par excellence.

A small falls and plunge pool terminates the stretch and gives way to a continuing succession of shallow cataracts, not worth your time. This ends in a narrow chute sliding under the Lower Iron Bridge and on into Ojo Caliente Bend, a deep, weed-filled curve that formerly hosted more big trout than any stretch on the Firehole. But during the late warming trend it became the hottest stretch of the river, topping 89 degrees on hot August days.

There are still many fish here, some quite large, and at the end of a hot summer one can find them packed into the lower end of Sentinel Creek, which enters at the very apex of the bend. These fish are very exposed in the clear, shallow water and are wild and wary. Most anglers find it useless to try for them and perhaps one shouldn't, as this stresses them and any additional stress in overwarm water decreases their chance of survival.

In Ojo Caliente Bend itself the abundant weeds make fishing difficult. This is true of all the weedy stretches, which includes all the slower, deeper waters from Biscuit Basin to the lip of the canyon. Also, insects in these weedy stretches tend to be small to microscopic and there are not many of them in Ojo Caliente Bend. Years ago, this piece of water was loaded with caddis and scud (shrimp, so called) but there are few of either that have survived the high temperatures of the 1970s. Now, small black snails form more than half the trout's diet. The fish are smaller and less plentiful than formerly, although by the standards of most trout streams the stock is adequate. But I've not caught a trout of three or more pounds here since 1976, before that they were common—though not commonly caught.

Below Ojo Caliente begins a long piece of water which traverses Fountain Flats and is called by that name. It is fairly even bottomed and its depth is also even, but there are some potholes and broken places in the bedrock bottom, though no really deep spots. The grass-covered banks are undercut throughout and this plus the potholes and some weeds furnish more holds for trout than at first appears. The water is a bit cooler than that of Ojo Caliente Bend.

In spring this is a favored piece of water, especially for the nymph fisher. A large dragonfly type is found here—and in other similar bottom types in the Firehole drainage. The nymph is in the water two years from egg to hatching adult and is tan to dark brown. It hatches into a fiery red-orange adult nearly three inches long.

I use my Assam Dragon pattern here in spring, in both its light and dark (tan and dark brown) phases and have excellent success. I have also caught many trout on other large (6 to 8, 2XL) nymph patterns. The old Gray Nymph has worked, although it in no way resembles the natural, and a size 6 or 8 Gold Ribbed Hare's Ear is first class.

In summer the Fountain Flats are the dry fly fishers bane—and delight. The water is truly wonderfully propitious for the dry fly, but this open meadow is often assaulted with winds up to fifty miles an hour. It has always been so. Ray Bergman, in the thirties, speaks of winds so strong that he had to aim his cast 45 degrees away from the river's edge in order to drop the fly along the bank where the fish were holding. But wind or no, this is a very popular piece of water in summer and early fall—grasshopper time— and the wind is a help here, blowing these ungainly creatures into the water and bringing the fish to feed.

From below Fountain Flats, below where the Nez Perce enters, to the breakover above the canyon head, is about three miles of excellent water: broad, smooth, well weeded, very tempting to the dry fly fisher. These are the Broads of the Firehole. Ernie Schwiebert allowed that they must have been so named by some of the Englishmen who early fly-fished these waters. They were named by me in 1948 and have been mentioned by that name several times in my writings. I also named Muleshoe Bend on this river.

At the very last before the river enters Firehole Canyon are a pair of long deep pools. They lie in the curve of the road where it returns to the river coming up from Madison Junction. These pools have very large boulders scattered through their otherwise even bottoms, and these boulders play havoc with the nymph fisher. They entangle his line and leader as he attempts to get down to the fish, which he must do since they will not come up to the fly. I have never taken more than one fish any day from these deep pools, although I have fished them often. But the fish are all large and well worth one's effort. Try them with a floating or sink tip line, long leader to 3X with some weight on the last eighteen inches, and a number 6 or 8 Hare's Ear nymph.

The Firehole Canyon is beautiful, with pools, flats, runs, rapids, cascades and falls, but except for the last half-mile before it joins the Gibbon and becomes the Madison, it is not worth the trouble and danger of getting into and out of the canyon to fish it.

The last half-mile has run-up fish from the Madison as well as resident fish of decent size. The giant stone fly nymph is found here, and in early June the adult, the so-called salmonfly, is found in sufficient numbers to make for some exciting dry fly fishing. You must hit it exactly right because the hatch only lasts two or three days on this short stretch and the date varies with the weather: In an early warm, dry spring the hatch may come before the May 28 opening of trout fishing in the Park.

The Firehole, in spite of its late temperature tribulations, is still a magnificent trout stream, challenging and difficult as it has always been. It is beautiful and it is unique; the hot springs, geysers and other thermal features that cause its temperature problems also make it minerally rich, which benefits the creatures in it greatly. These thermal features lining its banks have caused both Ernie Schwiebert and *National Geographic* magazine to call it the strangest trout stream on earth. I guess that makes it official.

NATURALS AND ARTIFICIALS

The temperature change in the Firehole has also changed the insect structure of the stream. Aquatic insects, like trout, are easily affected by temperature changes, and the larger ones are more affected than the smaller types. So in most cases it is the larger nymphs that are no longer found, or are much scarcer than they once were.

Pteronarcys and *Calineuria*, the big stone flies, are now rare and occasional. *Siphlonurus* and *Isonychia* mayflies appear gone. There are few large caddis. *Baetis*, the Blue Dun, is still found many places. *Ephemerella lacustris* is here but not in its former numbers.

Rhyacophila, *Brachycentrus*, *Chimarra* and other caddis forms are less plentiful but still present.

The dragon and damsel nymphs alone are present in their former numbers or nearly so. These two are found around the world in warm water as well as cold and are among the most resistant to temperature changes. Scud (fresh water shrimp, *Hyalella*) are now sparse and scattered.

There were formerly some riffle beetle larva in the Firehole (*Dytiscus*) but I haven't found any lately and they never were too plentiful. Blackfly and midge still abound. These small to microscopic forms are considered a nuisance by some, but the fish love them.

So you will need, as usual, the caddis dries, Elk Hair or Colorado King in 14, 16 and 18 and even 20. Soft-hackle wets with brown, gray or green bodies in 12, 14 and perhaps 16, will be useful. The Adams in all the above sizes is a must. For the mayflies, I've found Blue Dun, Blue Winged Olive and perhaps White Winged Black (*Tricorythodes*) in 16 and 18 for the first two, 22 for the latter fly, the most needed.

Some number 4 or 6, 2XL tan or brown dragon and damsel nymph patterns are useful and the old Gray Nymph in 6, 2XL is good, though I've found nothing it resembles.

You'll always need the big dries, in size 10, Royal Wulff, Hair Wing Variant, Grey Fox Variant (very good) and Renegade for the times when the trout are not showing. I've also caught many a fine trout on the Firehole with a Deerhair Mouse, although all my friends jeer at me for using it.

There are neither fish nor minnows other than trout in the Firehole and streamers are not much used. But hopper patterns from mid-July to the end of September are the best bet to raise more fish and bigger fish now that the hatches are fewer and the insects scarcer.

There are good-sized trout still left in the river, but catching them is a patience-testing act. I know of no trout anywhere warier than these.

Upper Falls of the Yellowstone River.

7
Gibbon River

Grebe Lake lies 8,000 feet up in the heart of Solfatara Plateau. It nestles in a small pocket basin, heavily timbered with the ever-present lodgepole pine on the north and east shores, with meadows on the west and south slopes. Ray Bergman has referred to it as "the most beautiful isolated trout pond I know." It is the source of the Gibbon River.

From the outlet on the southwestern corner of the lake the tiny headwaters stream meanders and winds through the dense lodgepole forest to Wolf Lake, about a mile (airline) away. It drops southward from Wolf Lake, loops, winds and twists because of the shallow gradient of the plateau, then drops suddenly over the escarpment, plunges through a narrow canyon and comes into view under the Norris-Canyon road bridge at the head of Virginia Meadows.

Virginia Meadows is about a mile-long meadow area covered densely with tall grass and spotted with clumps of dwarf willow, bitterbrush and mountain heath. The tiny creek looping, folding and winding across this canyon-walled bench is one of the loveliest meadow brook trout streams. It holds rainbows as well, but the icy waters and sparse insect supply cause it to be a panfishery. It is a delightful place to bring the family and a huge picnic lunch, and for children to fly-fish.

Below the Meadows the river plunges over Virginia Cascade and down into another of the narrow canyons that periodically pinch and confine this small clear stream. It leaves the Loop Road (the old Norris-Canyon road) and retreats into the lodgepole wilderness, coming into view again under the bridge at the head of Norris Meadows. It is a little larger here and a bit more fishworthy, but still very much a panfish affair. Through Norris Meadows the river winds, becoming larger from the input of Solfatara

Creek and several other smaller unnamed streams and the overflow of thermal features from the Norris Geyser Basin. These latter warm and enrich the water, and both the stream and the fish profit from it. The stream ducks behind the geyser basin's western edge, drops over a series of cascades and enters Elk Park. Here it is a full-blown trout stream.

Elk Park, and Gibbon Meadows, a mile further on, are the homes of many elk that graze, mate and give birth here. In September and October the courting and mating takes place. The bulls gather their harems and send their ringing challenges piercing the clear air and bouncing from the peaks. The young bachelors linger in the pods of lodgepole scattered throughout and peer jealously out at their more successful brethren. Both mating bulls and frustrated bachelors can be dangerous, so go warily in Elk Park and Gibbon Meadows at this time.

In Elk Park and Gibbon Meadows the Gibbon is a typical winding small meadow stream, with some weed beds and undercut banks providing holds for fish that are sometimes larger than one expects. I've not seen one here much larger than two pounds, but knowledgeable angling friends have on occasion seen them upwards of five. A trout that size in the open water of this small stream would look like a battleship.

From Gibbon Meadows, or rather just below, it is all downhill to near the confluence of the Firehole. The exception is at the lower end of the meadows. Here there are several deep pools in succession bending around through the lodgepoles to come again into sight and to join the road. In the meadows, one will have best luck with high-riding dries and hopper patterns from mid-July on. Here, in these pools, one wants the soft-hackle wets, a streamer such as Spruce, and the caddis dries.

Below Gibbon Falls, at its very foot, is a fine plunge pool that holds good trout most always, with an occasional lunker. The pool and next quarter-mile of pocket water is an excellent spot if you don't mind the climb into and out of the canyon. Do this a half-mile or so below the falls and work up and back down. The climb there is much safer and easier.

Beyond here to the confluence of the Firehole, the Gibbon is a typical riffle-and-run mountain stream with fairly long stretches of barren water. I like to work up a mile or two at a time, using a 12 Grey Fox Variant or Hair Wing Variant, then come back down the other side of the river with a Martinez Black nymph or my own Ida May in size 10. I move along quite rapidly, moving several steps between casts and skipping the shallow riffles. This small stream does not have many spots that require extensive searching with the fly.

In National Park Meadows, the Gibbon and Firehole join to become the Madison, a great and noted river, which we take up in the next chapter. This meadow stretch extends nearly a mile back up the Gibbon and for a very short distance into the mouth of Firehole Canyon. Since it is contiguous with the upper Madison, we will treat it as part of that river.

Gibbon Meadows area.

Gibbon Falls.

Elk Park area.

Downstream from Gibbon Falls.

NATURALS AND ARTIFICIALS

The insect structure of the Gibbon is less complex and the insects less numerous in genera and species than that of either the Firehole or the Madison. Except for not plentiful dragon-damsel types, the insects are mostly small. *Brachycentrus* and *Rhyacophila* caddis, and some net-spinning smaller forms are found. Stone flies are rare and scattered. *Epeorus* mayfly nymphs are found in the riffles below the falls and some *Ephemerella* and *Siphlonurus* in quieter waters, but all in all they are never plentiful.

For artificials the big, showy dries, Goofus, Royal Wulff, Hair Wing Variant and Renegade in 10 or 12 are much used. Blue Dun or Blue Winged Olive in size 16 is now and then needed. The Elk Hair Caddis or Colorado King in 14 and 16 will handle most caddis situations.

And of course, always have plenty of hopper patterns. These, and a selection of wingless wet flies with gray, green, orange and tan bodies, will cover most any need on the Gibbon where choice of fly is not critical.

Island Meadows area at dawn on the Upper Madison.

8
Madison River

It was in National Park Meadows where the Gibbon and Firehole come together to form the Madison that the Langford-Washburn-Doane (August–September 1870) expedition conceived the idea of making the area a national park. It was the world's first and it came to be in less than two years (March 1, 1872) after it was proposed to Congress. For this, and to the farsighted men of this expedition, we should be eternally grateful.

As mentioned earlier, these large meadows extend upstream nearly a mile along the Gibbon and a shorter distance up into the mouth of Firehole Canyon.

Roads come in from Old Faithful along the Firehole from the south, from Norris Junction along the Gibbon from the northeast, and from West Yellowstone to the west to form Madison Junction. All three of these roads run parallel and close to these streams, making them among the most accessible trout streams in the world.

The meadows lie in a flat bench in a broad canyon, and the water is typically large meadow stream with large deep pools and runs. There are tremendous beds of aquatic weeds, deeply undercut banks and numerous potholes to provide cover and holding places for trout. Formerly, this stretch held many three- to five-pound trout, but though some are still there, they are fewer due to warming of the water.

This warmth is due to the warming of the Firehole, which provides over 70 percent of the volume of the Madison at this point. The Firehole also supplies mineral richness, silicates for the building of diatoms—algae, the cell walls of which are formed of silica—and calcium bicarbonate which is used by plants, insects and trout in quantity. The Madison in the Park has over one hundred parts per million of calcium bicarbonates, thus is as rich in this mineral as most chalk streams.

The confluence of Gibbon River (far left) and Firehole River (far right) form the Upper Madison (foreground). Part of National Park Mt. is on the right (above). Big Bend (below).

Because of the weeds (*Potamogeton, Cerratophylum* and *Myriophylum*) this stretch is mostly dry fly fishing, or the emergent nymph can be used. At the very elbow of Big Bend, mentioned below, is a great deep pool which must be fished with nymphs along the bottom. The fish here simply will not come up to the fly.

In hopper season, those patterns fished along the banks and between the weed beds are the best bets because of the juicy splat! they make when they hit the water. The fish can hear or feel this and it brings them out of hiding among the weeds or from under the banks to assault this bonus with a spray-shattering rise.

The river swings away from the Madison Junction—West Yellowstone road about a half-mile from its headwater, over to near the south edge of the Madison Plateau and Three Brothers Peaks. National Park Mountain is the north-facing eastern rampart of the plateau, looming over the spot where the Langford-Washburn-Doane party sat around a campfire and dreamed of a national park.

The river swings back to the road about two miles from Madison Junction at the western (downstream) end of what is known to fishermen as Big Bend. The river is squeezed between high banks and the current accelerates around a couple of right-left curves and shoots down a three-quarter-mile-long riffle that holds few trout worth the anglers time. There is a deep spring hole across the river where it rejoins the road and a nine-pound brown was taken here once upon a time, and there is still a lunker or two in this spot.

Beyond the riffle is a short bench meadow section where the river divides around islands. Weeds, deep undercut banks and potholes in the bottom provide excellent holding for large trout. I remember one September day when a frosting of snow lay on the infacing slopes of the narrowing canyon, Joe Johnson and I took over thirty fish averaging two pounds, on nymphs, dry flies and large, bright steelhead patterns.

A short, deep run is followed by another small meadow stretch, then a half-mile-long riffle, mostly unfishworthy, leads into a curving run that ends at upper Nine Mile Hole. This curving run holds only panfish most of the summer and fall. But when the browns are running—now usually October because of the warming of the water—one can get into many trout and large trout in this run. Ernie Schwiebert and Gene Anderegg ran the numbers of trout over three pounds into double figures on this run one cold, snowy September, and some of the fish topped five pounds.

Nine Mile Hole is the best piece of trout holding water I've ever seen. It is a quarter-mile-long broad, deep run, with left-curving bends at both upper and lower ends. It has weeds, clear deep channels, gravel stretches, boulder and rubble stretches, flats, logs and drifts, silt beds and a 58-degree cold spring inlet on the far side of the upper middle of the run. I have never seen any piece of water that contained so many things necessary to a trout's welfare.

In the food category, it has three or four species of *Ephemerella* (some are now *Drunella*) including *Drunella grandis*, the Western Green Drake. It has a few *Siphlonurus*, *Trycorythodes* and *Centroptilum*, perhaps *Baetis*, and maybe others. It has *Brachycentrus*

Near Island Meadow area on the Upper Madison.

and *Rhyacophila* and other caddis, *Pteronarcys* and *Callineuria* (formerly *Acroneuria*) in stone flies, plus dragon and damsel flies. In short, a trout Eden. In the 1930s, when the limit was fifteen fish, a West Yellowstone angler took—and kept—fifteen trout from here totaling seventy-four pounds, about one ounce shy of five pounds per fish.

From lower Nine Mile Hole to Seven Mile Bridge is a huge marsh that is *very* dangerous. One can simply go over his waders in silt-filled potholes, along the bank as well as in the stream. I would not fish this treacherous area for all the gold in Fort Knox. I advise you not to, either.

Seven Mile Run commences a few feet above Seven Mile Bridge, the only bridge over the Madison in the Park. It and Nine Mile Hole are so named because they are these distances from the Park's west entrance.

The Run reaches for a half-mile down around a big curve, flanked by a steep lodgepole slope on the right, with the road and a picnic area on the left. It has many weedbeds with channels between, tree drifts and other debris, huge boulders and ledges. It is choice and challenging. I believe the trout to be more elusive and difficult here than anywhere else on the entire river.

Running from the curve ending the Run, for over a half-mile stretches famous Grasshopper Bank, named by Dave Whitlock (who loves it dearly as do many other noted anglers, including venerable Art Flick). It is a long, fairly deep, many-channeled run, the channels being grooves between hillocks and ridges of weed beds. It is most tricky to wade. One may stand knee deep on one of the weed-bed ridges, take a single step and be up to his armpits. Light conditions here are murderous. Though the current is quite moderate, I use a wading staff to probe ahead before taking that next step.

Grasshoppers abound in July through September on the sloping grass- and sagebrush-covered right bank that gave the run its name. Also in this spot, in August and September, one will encounter hatches of *Dicosmoecus atripes* caddis, the Great Orange Sedge. This or an orange-bodied hopper will produce well until the first heavy fall snow.

There is a damlike breakover at the end of this stretch, just where the new road swings away from the river, although the old road down along the three-mile stretch, known as Long Riffle, still is open to traffic. This riffle is almost purely a spawning and nursery stretch.

Coming in from West Yellowstone, six-tenths of a mile into the Park, a road turns left, running narrowly and inconsequentially through the lodgepoles, around a curve, dropping down a little hill, across the flat to the river. Here begins three miles of truly excellent wet fly and nymph water. The first stretch, at the parking area across from a rocky bluff, is locally called Hole Number One, and the entire stretch is called "the Barns Holes," due to the fact that stagecoaches, horses and, later, busses, were kept here for trundling people into the Park. All are gone now, but the name remains.

To the left, downstream three-eighths of a mile, is Hole Number Two, a parking area and end of the road. Still another three-eighths of a mile by foot is Hole Number

Grasshopper Bank area of the Upper Madison. Angler—Ernie Schwiebert.

A Great Blue Heron in the Long Riffle area of the Upper Madison.

Above Seven Mile Bridge where the Upper Madison comes out of the Swamp area (top). Madison Plateau is in the background.

Grasshopper Bank area of the Upper Madison.

Baker's Hole at daylight on the Upper Madison. Angler—Jack Gartside.

Three, the last of the *locally* named or numbered holes, which in fact are deep, fast runs. There are actually seven or eight of these from Cable Car Run just above Hole Number One, to the Beaver Meadows about three miles downstream. But only the first three are named by locals because, in the 1920s when the limit was twenty-five fish, it wasn't necessary to go beyond Hole Number Three to fill your limit.

Most of the fishing spots have been named by visiting fishermen. None, to my knowledge, have been named by the Park administration, which named everything else hereabouts. I make this point because if you ask a ranger or other Park personnel, "Where is the Greeny Deep?" all you'll get is a blank look.

The predominant insect throughout this stretch, and for most of the Madison all the way to Ennis, is *Pteronarcys californica*, the giant stone or "salmon" fly. There are also many *Calineuria californica*, the yellow stone fly. The big *Pteronarcys* nymphs are about two inches long at maturity, the *Calineuria* about two-thirds as large. These nymphs are in the water four and three years respectively from egg to emerging adult. They outweigh *all* other insects in the stream and form the greatest portion of the trout's food supply. Thus, an artificial representing them is the best day-in, day-out fly to use.

This heavy fast water is best fished with a sinking line (Hi-D), a leader of two feet and not less than OX and a size 4, 4XL weighted black nymph or Black Woolly Worm. Some streamers, Spruce, Green or Brown Marabou Muddlers or sculpin imitations are used with success. Sylvester Nemes fishes this water with a floating line, long leader and a number 6 or 8 soft-hackle wet fly, and does well. But Syl has been learning and developing this kind of wet fly fishing—the "greased line" method, for twenty-five years. He'd do well with any fly type.

The fast choppy water ends at the Beaver Meadows, a marshy, boggy, beaver-tunneled, willow-clumped area about five river miles long that ends at Baker's Hole at the Park boundary. This is mostly flat water, pools, glides, flats, with an occasional short, fast stretch. It is predominately dry fly water, although the big dragonfly nymphs will work at times.

From the broad depths of Baker's Hole, where there is a state campground, on into Hebgen Lake, is the stamping ground of the "gulper" fishermen, those sly and secretive fellows and gals who gather here at dawn or sometimes dusk to fish very tiny dry flies for nice large trout. They use float tubes, canoes, kayaks, punts, cartop boats and, occasionally, cabin cruisers to pursue their elusive quarry. There are days when no hatch develops and no fish come and those are the days that I have tried this form of trout madness. It did not grow on me.

The water coming from the tailrace of Hebgen Dam is always around 40 degrees, and for the next two miles, to the head of Quake Lake, this water is warmed just enough to make the trout happy. Because of stable flow and temperature, this is the most predictable stretch of the river. I usually open the season here, and even then (late May) one can get dry fly fishing with the Elk Hair Caddis.

The water comes raging over the slide dam of Quake Lake, roars down a long,

The Lower Madison between Hebgen and Quake Lakes.

Baker's Hole at dawn on the Upper Madison.

narrow chute and pours foaming into the Slide Inn Run. This is choice water, with many trout and large trout. It is loaded with insects—the big stone flies, several mayfly species, many caddis, crane fly larvae and sculpins. This was so even before the 1959 earthquake that created Quake Lake. I have never been able to find what it is that makes this such a propitious stretch for insects, for large trout—and for huge whitefish, the biggest I've seen anywhere in the area.

There is a small store–gas station and R.V. park here, called, naturally, Slide Inn. John and Ann Reed spent the summer of 1982 here in their trailer. Ann was just getting into nymph fishing and worked the water daily with the big stone fly nymphs, learning her trade. John and friends were having very good dry fly fishing for fish up to seventeen inches and when Ann would come in at the end of the day with no success to report, they would urge her to give up. But she changed their tune a bit when she came in to report, on separate days, that she had taken browns of nineteen and twenty-three inches out of the raging waters. An instant interest in nymph fishing was created.

From the U.S. Highway 87 bridge over the river, down to Varney Bridge (about thirty-five miles of river), the water is much the same—long riffles with a few somewhat deeper runs. It is boulder- and rubble-bottomed fast water fishing that offers good fishing, excellent really, since it was changed to a no-kill area five years ago. But it does not offer great variety of choice of water type or tactics.

The Big Bend section about a mile below the Cliff–Wade Lake Bridge is superb pocket water dry fly fishing, usually with smaller caddis patterns. I have friends who, having to work for a living, can only get here in summer after five o'clock. But between then and dark, about ten-thirty in this area, they often take twenty trout averaging close to seventeen inches, with seldom anything under fifteen. This kind of thing can become addictive.

Though there are favorite spots all along this stretch, they are similar enough to require the same flies and methods—caddis dries, the big rough water dries, stone fly nymphs and some streamers. It usually takes trial and error to arrive at the taking method.

Some favored spots are the end-of-road area on the left bank three or so miles above the West Fork, spot sections of deeper water all the way down and the piece above and below the West Fork Bridge.

The five-mile section from Wolf to Squaw Creek was for some years a special study section closed to fishing. The results of this continuing study are used to maintain or improve the fishery in the rest of the river and in other streams in Montana. The area is now open—and the fishing is splendid.

There are campgrounds at Palisades and Ruby Creek, and a boat launching place at McAtee Bridge on this stretch. From McAtee on to Varney the river begins to assume a different character, with deeper water that is boulder filled and good throughout. Here, to insure success, one must be thorough and cover the water, because there are many

Looking upstream on the Lower Madison between Hebgen and Quake Lakes. The old cabin on the right was moved by the earthquake.

Above Raynold's Pass (Highway 87) Bridge on the Lower Madison (above). The Lower Madison near McAtee with a natural Salmon Fly and Bird's Stone Fly Artificial (below).

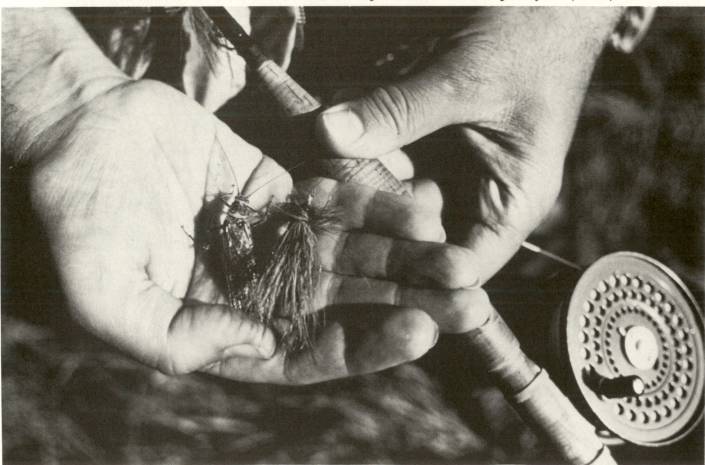

Near West Fork on the Lower Madison. Angler—Jim Nelson.

large trout in this stretch and there is no way for the angler to tell just where they are lying.

Below Varney Bridge this deepening of the water continues, making it harder to judge where the fish are, but the dividing of the river around islands (the Channels) gives the fisherman a somewhat more manageable piece of water to work. I would earnestly advise taking a guide the first one or two times the angler fishes this part of the Madison. Very good guides are available at West Yellowstone and at Ennis. You'll get in a bit more fishing time on the Varney-Ennis stretch if you headquarter at Ennis. The same applies to the Slide Inn–Varney water; you'll save time by staying at West Yellowstone if you're going to float the river.

The major nymph in this entire section—Slide Inn to Ennis—is the giant stone fly nymph and one of the more than twenty representations of this nymph is the best day-in, day-out medicine. During the emergence or "hatch" of this insect, the so-called salmon-fly, there will be millions of these two-inch-long adults all along the bank for miles. When the hatch is well under way, one must locate the "head" of the hatch, the half-mile or so area where the fish are not taking the nymphs as they move to shore to crawl out, or where they are not yet glutted on the adults. It can be difficult to find the head of the hatch, but if you do you can have a day's fishing you simply will not believe.

Two years ago, Koke Winter and I drifted in his cartop boat into "the head of the hatch." There were only a few adults flying around, more as the day progressed. It was mid-June, the river was very high and strong, but clear. We got into over forty fish that day, mostly in the yard or so of quieter water along the banks. Many times we had to cast sixty feet to get the fly over and would get only a 2-foot drift before the fly started to skip across on the choppy currents. That was where the trout would catch up to and smash the fly in a savage, slashing take. When we set the hook, the fish simply shifted into overdrive and headed for Ennis Lake. That day the reels actually screamed. And chattered and clattered and rattled and fell apart. About four in the afternoon, the line guard of my old 1495 Pfleuger Medalist fell into the stream, the frame screws vibrated out and followed it, and the nearly empty spool shot out into my line hand. There I was, a four- or five-pound trout securely on at the end of 150 feet of line and an OX leader, and a wrecked reel. I lost that fish, had two others as large or larger straighten out my number 4, 4XL *regular* wire English hooks. And one of at least six pounds broke my leader. Koke and I landed only those fish under three pounds (but not much under). When we left the stream at dark, we vibrated, jerked and twitched all the way back to West Yellowstone.

That's the way it can be on the lower middle Madison during the salmonfly hatch, mid-June to mid-July. But first you have to locate the head of the hatch. And be sure your reel screws, if any, are seated in with Pliobond. Mine are—now.

Near Ennis on the Lower Madison. Angler—Charles Brooks.

The Slide Inn area of the Lower Madison.

NATURALS AND ARTIFICIALS

We have covered herein about eighty miles of the Madison River. Some of those miles are vastly different water than other miles, so the insect life is different. I'll do my best to sort it out for you.

In the Park, you will find *Siphlonurus occidentalis; Drunella grandis; Ephemerella inermis, infrequens* and *lacustris;* several *Baetis,* all similar; *Tricorythodes,* and *Centroptilum* among the mayflies. These are, respectively, Gray Drake (size 10), Western Green Drake (size 10), Pale Morning Dun (size 16), Blue Dun and Blue Winged Olive (size 16), White Winged Black (size 20), and White Winged Sulphur Drake (size 22).

There are many species of *Brachycentrus* and *Rhyacophila* caddis in the entire river. Colorado King, gray body and green body, and Elk Hair Caddis, brown body or gray body, in sizes 14, 16 and 18, will handle nearly all these situations. You'll need Great Orange Sedge or Bucktail Caddis, orange body, size 8, 2XL for this hatch (check Appendix A for hatch times of all insects herein). Caddis appear in all areas of gravel bottom.

Pteronarcys californica and *Calineuria californica* are needed in both dry fly and nymph patterns. Check Appendix B for names and sizes, as well as hatch times in Appendix A.

Dragon and damsel patterns are less important on this river. They will really only be needed in Big Bend in National Park Meadows, in the Beaver meadows section and in Baker's Hole. A brown and tan dragonfly nymph (size 4, 2XL) and a brown damsel nymph (size 8, 3XL) will see you through for both these.

You'll need hoppers, one of those in Appendix B, for the entire river. You'll also need Royal and Grey Wulff, Goofus Bug and either Renegade or Hair Wing Variant (House and Lot) in size 10 as general dry flies.

For wets, other than the big stone fly nymphs, you should have Martinez Black or Ida May, size 10 (entire river); Gray Nymph, size 8 (in the Park); soft-hackle patterns in 12 and 14 with gray, brown, yellow or green bodies. (See the list in Appendix B.)

If it pleases you, the big streamers, Regular and Dark Spruce, Green or Brown Marabou Muddlers, a good sculpin pattern and an Olive Matuka, in sizes 2 through 2/0 will be found useful.

Near Rockhaven. Angler—Don Kast.

9
Gallatin River

This is another river, of several, which is very easy to approach in its most fishable and fishworthy stretches. It runs beside a major north-south roadway for most of its length. That is U.S. 191 from West Yellowstone to Three Forks, although we do not go so far afield. Our coverage ends at Gallatin Gateway, because the river below here, although it still contains trout and some very large trout, runs almost entirely through private property. The stream was the first river in Montana to be declared by the courts as navigable, therefore the banks below the high-water line, and the streambed, are public. Still, this section offers problems that the others do not, one of which is that it was much abused, even de-watered, before the court decision.

The Gallatin rises in two branches on the north face of Three Rivers Peak in Yellowstone Park. In a short distance, these two feed into Gallatin Lake, out of which the river emerges, still above 9,500 feet and very cold. It first comes into view at Milepost 22 (from West Yellowstone) where it is joined by the waters of Fan Creek from the north, Divide Creek from the south, and just a bit further on, by Bacon Rind Creek from the west. These three more than double the flow and quickly make the Gallatin into a mountain trout stream. Though it runs through a pastoral valley for many miles, it is not a meadow stream. It is composed almost entirely of riffles and runs; there are few pools in the next thirty miles and few large fish. It is mostly a panfish stream here and a pure pleasure to fish. There are few places in these thirty miles where the angler cannot cast across without strain. It can also be waded without difficulty, the round, smooth, but not slick, gravel-rubble bottom requires only felt soles, and few places cannot be waded in hippers.

Middle section of the river.

This is quite a cool stream and because of the lake and characteristics of the watershed, is stable in temperature and comfortable for the trout, rainbows and cutthroat in this upper section. It is only moderately mineral rich and well supplied with oxygen. The mayfly and caddis that dwell in its singing riffles are small and not overly plentiful. The trout often look to the surface for terrestrial food in summer.

From where it first comes into sight until it enters the Gallatin Canyon it is seldom out of sight and, though it grows larger, it never changes its character. It is an open, pleasant, riffle-loaded little river that stimulates but never really challenges. In the Canyon and beyond, it is an entirely different stream.

This section is not for hard work or hard fishing. On those days when you wish to pleasantly relax and enjoy the out-of-doors, some lovely, restful scenery, and fish a friendly stream with light tackle, hie yourself to the Gallatin at Milepost 22 and beyond.

This section is much favored by animals, which do not interfere with the fishermen but do add interest to the landscape by creating a wilderness aspect even though the highway is right beside you.

To fish this stretch, take along a big lunch, perhaps a pleasant libation, and park along any stretch that suits your mood for the day. You can fish up with the dry fly or terrestrials and back down with small wets or nymphs. The trout are not many nor large but they are friendly and willing, and you will have a relaxing, pleasant day on one of the friendliest rivers in the West. It's open countenance is just as it seems, it holds no secrets from you. The fish are where you think they are and you fish it as you think you should. No stream can be more honest than that.

The canyon section is a big, rough, brawling mountain river, surging toward its junction with the Madison and Jefferson. It is boulder filled and boisterous, difficult to fish and to wade. There are occasional short channels or runs, but by and large this is pocket water. Many of its strong riffles lack the depth to be good holding water, but one will find fish in them at times. When they are in such shallow stretches, they are there to feed, but they are not there often nor for long periods.

This type water begins about Milepost 49 and continues for the next fifteen miles. The gradient is generally steep, but there are some benches that cause a long (200- to 300-yard) flat-water stretch with a fast chute at the head and another at the foot. These rare spots provide some dry fly fishing that at times is excellent. Even when the fish are not feeding or insects hatching, one can still do well at the end and around the sides of the upper fast-water tongue, and in the "tail of the flat," as Gene Connett called it in his lovely book.

There is much pocket water which can be successfully fished with the dry fly, and down here in the canyon, the fish are larger. But there is not much running room, so most times a leader of 3X is sufficient with the high-floating dry or the hopper pattern.

This is stone fly water and day-in, day-out, the big black nymph imitations will produce the larger trout, though not the greatest number. Here one wants a sink tip line, or even a full floater, because of the boulders. Also, one needs a short leader, two feet or

Upper section of the river.

Near Westfork area. Angler—Don Kast.

so, and a heavily weighted nymph. One fishes as short a cast as possible, holds the rod tip up and "steers" the fly alongside or through the pocket. The trout in such water hit the nymph with a smash. The leader must not be finer than 1X, and 0X is better.

The better fishing is a little distance from, or out of sight of, the many parking spots. We're not talking of great distances here—a hundred yards or so out of sight of the road or any open area will find undisturbed water. Wear your felt-sole chest waders, cross over and fish the side away from the highway and you can find trout that do not see one angler a year.

The water here is not the friendly riffle water above Milepost 49. It is very strong and fast, it means you no harm but will not stand for poor footing or slippery soles. The bottom is rough and of stones piled on stones. But it is not dangerous if you mind your business and do not wade (move) and fish *at the same time*. Do one or the other but not both and you'll be all right.

If one locates at the Greek Creek area or at Karst's Ranch, you will have found that these divide the canyon stretch roughly in thirds. However, it is no more than a thirty-minute drive from either place to the halfway point between them, or between Karst's and West Yellowstone.

There are mountain sheep on the mountains and the canyon walls above the river and in May and sometimes June the sheep will come down along the river, giving one a rare glimpse of these creatures of the high places. One can also encounter moose or elk anywhere on this stream.

The canyon stretch requires that the fly-fisher do some thinking before and while fishing. The stretches of water, at first glance, may appear quite similar to one another, but closer examination will reveal that is not so and that these stretches are, in fact, quite variable. This means that a little study of how to fish each stretch *before* it is fished will increase one's chances.

Unless there is a hatch on, the dry fly fisher will have more success with the big general floaters. The Goofus Bug in size 10 or 12 is nearly always a good producer, more so here than in other places. Hoppers from June through September are a good choice, ants and a size 12 Colorado King or Elk Hair Caddis in August do a good job. It is presumed that the latter flies imitate the adult of the spruce budworm, which regularly infests the forests through which the river runs in the Canyon.

In June there is the salmonfly hatch and one can do yeoman work with the floating adult. As is true anywhere this hatch occurs, one must seek out the head of the hatch where the fish are feeding fully on the egg-laying flyers and not on the crawling nymphs. I like to locate this feeding area by driving slowly down the highway from well above, where there are no flyers yet, and continue until I see several in the air at one time. Since the road and river are often side by side and never far apart, this is the lazy man's way of doing things. Once parked, with rod in hand, go to the river and watch intently for feeding fish. If none are showing and you have chosen your stopping place correctly, you *should* find the fish feeding a little farther downstream. Move steadily down the bank,

Upper section.

looking for flies in the air, especially on the water, and signs of feeding fish. When you see all three from where you stand, you have "found the place."

About six or so miles from Gallatin Gateway, the road comes out of the canyon, crossing from your right to your left under the bridge as you proceed downstream. The river now begins to change character completely. Gone are the boulder-lined pockets and surging currents. The land is much flatter and the river slows down and begins to be a stream of long runs and deep pools. There is still some faster water, generally where one pool ends and the next begins, but this is calmer, deeper water for the most part.

The fish in the deep pools are often quite large, though never plentiful. They are mostly taken on bait, though a big dragon nymph worked slowly with twitches along the bottom on a sinking line and short leader will bring up a big brown once in a while. A leech (ugh!) will also work if you can abide the brutes (artificial, of course).

Excellent dry fly fishing can be had if you know where to fish. The trout feeding on the surface here locate themselves differently than on any other stream of the area. Rich McIntyre, who reclaims trout streams for a living (Timberline Reclamations, for which I am a consultant), lived on this stretch of the river near Gallatin Gateway for many years. It took him a few of those years to learn where the fish were feeding on the surface. They are nearly always found in the shallow tail of the faster runs—not in the deeper water near the head and not in the quieter water alongside the current tongue, but in the flat water just before the next run or pool begins. This water is choppy and it is difficult to see the fish take the fly, natural or artificial. But once you have found where the fish are, you can do well, and occasionally run into a lunker that has sneaked in among the yearlings.

In 1982, Ed Zern, George Harvey, Bucky Metz and I went down to spend an evening with Rich on this water that he knows so well. Rich outfished all of us for numbers, although George got into a fish of six or seven pounds that he wasn't expecting, and it cleaned him before he could get his act together. Since George is one of the world's best and most experienced fly-fishers for trout, it is comforting for us lesser lights to know that even the masters lose a big one now and then.

The fishing in this farmland area, with its huge cottonwood and other deciduous trees, and plentiful vines and underbrush along the bank, is more like eastern trout fishing in some of its aspects, than it is western mountain trout fishing, and easterners find that they feel right at home here. And they find that eastern flies and methods do quite well, which makes them quite happy. And happy is what trout fishing is all about.

NATURALS AND ARTIFICIALS

From Milepost 22 to Milepost 45 or thereabouts, the insects are mostly small and not plentiful in the Gallatin. (This river is often called the *West* Gallatin River; there is no such river. There is an East Gallatin near Bozeman and there is *the* Gallatin River—this one.) Mayflies are almost rare, I know of only two genera, *Epeorus* and *Ephemerella,* and I have never seen a significant mayfly hatch on this stretch. An Ida May or Martinez Black, size 10, will work fine for the nymphs of these two.

Caddis are more plentiful and, as usual, *Brachycentrus* and *Rhyacophila* are predominant, Elk Hair Caddis and Colorado King in sizes 12, 14 and 16 will handle most caddis hatches. There is a larger caddis scattered through this water, never plentiful, but the cinnamon-colored adult, size 10, causes an occasional feeding flurry. I use my Skunk Hair Caddis to simulate the cased larval form, which I have been unable to identify, and find Grey Fox Variant works well enough for the adult, although a size 10 Goddard Caddis looks much more like the natural.

Use green-, gray- or brown-bodied grouse-hackle wets to simulate the pupal caddis forms, sizes 12 and 14. Gold Ribbed Hare's Ear nymph in sizes 6, 8, 10 and 12 is the best all-around wet fly for this stretch of river.

Hoppers, ants and the big floaters, so often mentioned, round out the flies needed here.

The big stone fly nymph and salmonfly dry are useful along with the above patterns in the Canyon. Some also prefer the streamers, Spruce and Olive Matuka and perhaps others. A sculpin pattern is good.

The farmland section requires the big dragon nymph, the leech or Woolly Bugger, and the dry flies listed above. Insects are more plentiful here and somewhat more varied, but intelligent selection of the flies above should suffice except in very rare instances. The Light Cahill 12 and 14 is sometimes needed.

Rainbow Trout on Railroad Ranch.

10
Henry's Fork, Snake River

This river was discovered by white men in 1810 when a trappers' brigade led by Andrew Henry camped at Three Forks, where the Gallatin, Madison and Jefferson meet to form the Missouri, and were forced out by Blackfeet Indians. Henry led his brigade up the Madison, over Raynolds Pass near present Quake Lake Slide, past Henry's Lake and down along the river which was to bear his name. Henry was either the unluckiest or most incompetent trappers' brigade leader in history but the lake and river he discovered may just be the best trout stream and lake in the forty-eight lower states.

The lake, which is the source of the river, lies in a loop of the continental divide, which here is part of the wall of the Island Park Caldera, perhaps the largest collapsed volcanic caldera in the world. It is some twenty by thirty miles across, and the river meanders the entire length. The lake is fed by seven mostly snow- and rain-supplied creeks, and by icy springs in its bottom. It is very rich water for trout, loaded with weeds and insects. An idea of its quality may be gained from two facts: Trout of over 18 pounds have been caught there; and in the 1890s about 90,000 pounds of trout a year were harvested from the lake and sold commercially. One fly-fisher I know took more than one hundred trout of over 5 pounds *each* every summer from 1945 to 1970 from the lake. Most were not kept.

The river flowing from the outlet dam (which was put in in the early 1920s to raise the lake level for downstream irrigation) is just as rich as the lake. It winds across the grassy, often flower-blanketed meadows of Henry's Lake Flat, amongst the grazing cattle and sheep. This is a section of quiet runs and deep pools with often marshy or boggy banks and many spring-fed tributary creeks. The fish do not have many holding spots due to an almost featureless bottom, and tend to gather in the deeper pools. They are difficult to lure from these clear-water depths and are very much a stalking proposition. There are about six miles of this meadow-marsh water and then about two miles of dense willow swamp before the river meets the 480 million-gallon daily flow of 52 degree water from Big Springs.

Across the meadows one will encounter herds of antelope and mobs of sandhill cranes, as well as stilt, curlew, herons and numerous waterfowl. All attest to the undisturbed and unspoiled quality of land and water. In the willows the many moose give further evidence that this is an area where man and wildlife have come to terms with each other and coexist to the profit of both.

From Big Springs confluence down to the U.S. Highway 191 bridge at Mack's Inn the river is a deep swamp-marsh stream of very large pools with a mostly silt-covered bottom. There is gravel underneath the silt, and it shows in some places, but in others the silt is deep enough to be very troublesome.

The land surrounding the stream here is all private; part of the Island Park Summer Home area, and of several fishing clubs. The status of the river has never been established as navigable, therefore one wants to be careful not to trespass. You will find the people friendly if you yourself are courteous and considerate of property rights.

It is six or eight miles downstream to the head of Island Park Reservoir. The distance varies with the lake level. This is riffle-and-run water for the most part. There is a short, steep canyon between Upper and Lower Coffee Pot rapids. This canyon is called Cardiac Canyon by some, but the true Cardiac Canyon is miles downstream at the upper–lower Mesa Falls area. At times there will be huge rainbows in the deep water of the canyon, at other times only smaller fish will be taken.

This upper section, from McRae's Bridge at the head of the reservoir to the section at Mack's Inn, is regularly stocked with hatchery catchable trout for the tourist trade. This has disturbed the wild trout; in some cases they have been forced by the sheer weight of numbers to retreat to the reservoir. But now and then you can find a pod of sizable wild fish in the deeps between Mack's Inn and the confluence of Big Springs, and in the Upper and Lower Coffee Pot sections.

Above the confluence of Big Springs and on to the lake outlet is all wild trout. This section is the least fished of any part of the river. This is largely because it is approached by roads only at the Highway 191 bridge just below the outlet and by the road that cuts left off Highway 191 (going south) just at the edge of Henry's Lake Flat, past Island Park Lodge. Two hundred yards from either of these approaches the trout do not see one angler per five years. Yet there are three-pounders to be had by the careful and patient. This water and these trout cannot be rushed.

This six-mile meadow section is one of the most beautiful areas in the world. Here one fishes alone in a pastoral meadow flat ten miles across, flanked on three sides by mountain ranges in excess of 10,000 feet, with wild animals, birds and waterfowl all around. In the clear air the mountains appear so close that one might toss a rock and hit

Mesa Falls. Angler—Will Godfrey.

them, yet there is a wonderful feeling of airy openness.

Fishing the dragonfly nymph here will produce only spotty success, though the fish run large, seldom less than two pounds. But the better fishing is with terrestrials: hoppers, ants, cricket and beetle patterns. One must seek concealment or kneel while casting and keep low until the fish are hooked. Though not much fished for, if at all, by human anglers, the trout are preyed on constantly by ospreys, eagles and herons. So they are wary. But they can be taken, and for the angler who hates crowds and loves solitude in lovely surroundings, Henry's Lake Flat is the place.

The long, deep section between the Big Springs confluence and Mack's Inn can and does produce good hatches and rises and generally fish over a pound. If one can find an approach to the stream while avoiding trespass, this is truly excellent water. The hatches can be exasperating, for the silt bottom produces midge and blackfly by the millions and the trout feed lustily on these minute creatures. During these periods, which are the most common, a fly larger than size 20 is useless. Color or pattern is not important, but neutral colors do work best. I have a fly for this condition that has never failed me. It is the Peterson Palmer, size 20, with a body of the thinnest possible peacock herl and three turns of good grizzly dry fly hackle palmer style. It is easy to tie—if such tiny flies are— and it is the most effective fly for such hatches that I know of. It can be fished dry, in the film, or just sunken, by judicious use of power with the rod. Drop lightly for surface fishing, let it come down harder for in the film and spat it on the water to sink it.

This section of the river has rainbow, some cutthroat and many small brookies during the summer. In fall, big rainbows, some kokanee and coho salmon run up this far from Island Park Reservoir. The latter two *can* be taken on colorful wet flies, but it is not easy.

At Island Park Dam begins some twenty miles of the best fly-fishing for trout that can be found anywhere. The fish are in this stretch by the countless thousands and some will *top* twenty pounds. They are now all wild trout, no stocking is currently being done in this stretch and hasn't been for several years.

The spillway or tailrace of the dam feeds into the head of Box Canyon, the best fast-water stretch of trout fishing water in the country. There are about three miles of this fast, boulder-filled channel and pocket water and for the stouthearted angler it is a veritable cornucopia of riches and opportunities. The entire stretch is loaded with stone fly nymphs, at least three and perhaps five, species. There are a dozen species of caddis, several mayfly types, some crane fly larvae, and there are sculpins to fatten the huge, almost grossly fat rainbows that live here. I've seen rainbows out of this stretch not twenty-six inches long that weighed *over* ten pounds. About every two or three years a fifteen-pounder will be taken, and there are larger ones in the stream *all the time*.

The canyon is entered most easily by the road turning into the reservoir just above (north of) Pond's Lodge, then turning off just short of the dam down to the boat launching spot about a half-mile downstream from the tailrace. Both up and down stream of this access point is good fishing for larger than average fish and this section is more easily waded than the rest of the canyon downstream of the tributary Buffalo, which enters just below the boat launching spot. Stone fly nymphs are the best choice of fly 80 percent of the time. Big floaters and terrestrials, or streamers—Dark Spruce, Marabou Muddler or a sculpin pattern—take care of the other 20 percent.

There are several entry spots below here, none easy. One comes from Highway 191 to the bank just below the juncture with the Buffalo River. Then this road (dirt) proceeds downstream along and back from the edge of the canyon, where turnoffs and parking spots appear several times in the next three miles. One parks, gathers up his gear, hoists his wader belt, takes a deep breath and clambers down into the canyon, about 300 vertical feet in most places.

Once into the canyon, your troubles just begin. *Now*, you have to find a spot where you can wade out far enough from the canyon wall to make any kind of a cast. Trees and smaller growth push right down to the water. In the edge of the water, and throughout, are boulders. Some are just ankle high, some knee high, some crotch high, and there are bigger ones and smaller ones *passim*. But it is the ankle- and knee-high rocks that cause the problem. All intent on your lawful occasions, you will turn to step here, or there, or move straight ahead, your foot will catch a slippery boulder in midstep, shoot off at the speed of light and hurl you headlong into the stream. You *do not* wade and fish. First, you wade. Then you fish. Then you wade some more. And fish some more. And so on. Try wading and fishing and you'll wind up wet, gasping for breath after an icy dunking or maybe being plastered against a huge boulder thirty feet downstream after being tumbled around like a twig. To my knowledge, we've never lost an angler in Box Canyon. We've never had one fish it successfully without a dunking, either. Me? You bet, every time.

The big stone fly nymph is the first choice of fly and used most of the time. Streamers and big floaters come into play when the nymph unaccountably doesn't work. And in early June, the dry imitation of the salmon fly can produce a bewildering number of sizes of trout. I have caught them from six inches to six pounds from the same spot. Normally, six-inch and six-pound trout do not live together. But in salmonfly time everything is crazy—the trout, the insect, the anglers, the weather, even the tourists. I won't tell you to be careful, to keep your wits about you, because you won't anyway. But you'll have a hell of a time and you may hang a trophy.

Most of the canyon's three miles is very similar. Choice of location is by hunch, and usually one place is as good as the next. But the very mouth, where the water spills out from the walls of tumbled and broken rock and shoots down into the mile-long deep glide to Last Chance, is a special place. Let me tell you how special.

A friend of mine, Koke Winter, came by from West Yellowstone one dark, gloomy, late fall day on his way to fish "the Box" as we say locally.

"Bob Jacklin wants me to get him a good big rainbow to mount in his shop," Koke

Near the end of Box Canyon. Angler—Bill Mason.

Just above Railroad Ranch at Last Chance. Angler—Craig Mathews.

said. "I'd feel better about the chances if you went along."

But I was getting in my winter wood, the weather looked snowy, and I had to refuse.

Koke went down to this white-water deep at the mouth of the Canyon and in less than two hours landed two rainbows of over ten pounds each, taken on the big stone fly nymph.

In the summer of 1982, a local workman on his lunch hour landed a ten-pounder one day and an eighteen-pounder another day. But the local Fish and Wildlife agent, on seeing the latter fish, was not too impressed. "We shocked that hole this spring," he said. "There's a bigger fish, over twenty-four pounds, still there."

The deep, channeled, rocky-bottomed glide curving from the mouth of the canyon down to beyond Last Chance is flanked by summer homes and is full of nice trout. It is mostly wadable and a joy to fish with either nymph or dry fly. In order not to trespass, most anglers move up the broken blacktop road along the river and stop at a parking area near the first of the streamside cabins. Then they wade across and go up the trail along the far bank to where they wish to fish. The mouth of the canyon can be reached by this trail.

The lower end of the Last Chance Run ends at the upper end of Harriman State Park, the famed Railroad Ranch. Something more than five miles of water is included in the Park but the water just above and below Osborne Bridge is not usually meant when fishermen speak of the Ranch. The Ranch water is as good as any trout water anywhere. It is loaded with fish of every size up to, and perhaps over, twelve pounds. It is full of weed beds, deep channels, potholes, bays and inlets and contains more and more kinds of aquatic insects than any water I've ever seen.

On the nineteenth of June, 1978, I counted thirteen different species of insects on the water at one time. There were *Rhyacophila* and *Brachycentrus* caddis in five species, two species of *Baetis*, two of *Ephemerella*, one *Callibaetis*, some *Pteronarcys californica* left over from the main hatch, one *Ephemera* and a damselfly I couldn't identify. All these were in some stage or other of their adult life—some just emerging, some spent spinners, some laying eggs. The water was a metallic color from the insects that literally covered it. And the fish, glutted, were not feeding.

This is not that unusual a condition. Almost any day from late May (fishing in Harriman Park does not open till June 15 as of 1982) through November there will be several species of flies on the water at the same time. Some of these will invariably be midge and blackfly. And the fish seen feeding may not all be taking the same insect, and some may be taking the emerging nymph or larvae and not the winged adult. This kind of thing is frequent and will drive you right out of your mind. Also, to add to your frustration, the larger fish seem to prefer the smaller flies. My friend, Bob Holmes, a sly and secretive but top-drawer fly-fisher, took a trout of five or six pounds here a couple of years ago on a size 22 fly and a 7X leader. If you want to know how to handle such a fish

Just above Railroad Ranch at Last Chance. Angler—Bing Lempke.

Just above Railroad Ranch at Last Chance at dusk. Angler—Rene Harrop.

On Railroad Ranch (above). Rainbow Trout being released on Railroad Ranch (below).

on such terminal tackle, read "Murder," in *Fishless Days, Angling Nights,* by Sparse Grey Hackle.

The fishing water from the mouth of Box Canyon to Osborne Bridge will see perhaps 200 to 300 fly-fishers a day from June 15 to the end of July. These, for the most part, not only know how to fly-fish, they know the etiquette and seldom is there friction. Actually, there are enough trout and water for everyone, and a positive benefit is that someone in that crowd is going to find an answer and share it. You'll be glad for the help and, I think, to help, when you are the one who has solved the problem.

Below Osborne Bridge on down to the little rural subdivision of Pinehaven, about three miles of water, there are some nice glides, a riffle or two, then the long, curving smooth-water stretch athwart Pinehaven. You will find private property signs on the trees and by the roads of the subdivision. Like any such zoned area, the land is private, the roads and streets public. And this is fortunate, for the half or three-quarters of a mile of water just above and below Pinehaven is a truly fine stretch of water with almost as many insects as the Ranch.

The trout are not as plentiful, but there are quite enough, and some exceed twenty-four inches. The place is seldom fished, though boats launched at Osborne Bridge do float through the stretch. Of an evening, the dry fly fishing can be unbeatable.

Below here is a section of broken water, riffles and runs, some glides and some almost-rapids, all the way to Riverside Campground, where our coverage ends. This varied water calls for varied fishing methods, wet fly, dry fly, nymph and streamer. It is perhaps best reached by floating and stopping to fish the likely or more appealing places, of which there are many. It is something more than ten miles by river from Osborne Bridge to Riverside, and if you do your work well and cover only the water that appeals to you, it is a very full day's fishing. It is varied and challenging and often very rewarding—and that's true of all of Henry's Fork.

NATURALS AND ARTIFICIALS

Among the mayflies, *Baetis* species appear throughout the season, and one needs Blue Dun and Blue Winged Olive in sizes 14 through 22 to cover this important series of hatches. *Callibaetis,* the Speckled Dun and Spinner, size 14, hatches in different areas at different times mid-June through August and is handled by Slate Wing Olive number 14. *Drunella* (also formerly *Ephemerella*) *grandis,* the Western Green Drake, size 10, causes massive excitement from mid-June through mid-July; and the Brown Drake, *Ephemera simulans,* number 10, is intermixed with this hatch, but usually comes at different times of day.

The biggest hatches are those of *Ephemerella inermis, infrequens* and *lacustris*, the Pale Morning Dun number 16 or 18, which comes on May through July. Anglers will argue about which species is which, but entomologists have told me that *they* cannot tell one from the other without a magnifying glass. Since trout don't carry magnifying glasses, I lump these three together. *Pseudocloeon edmundsi*, the tiny Blue Winged Olive, size 22, will at times, from mid-July through October, cover the water like pollen. This is a terribly difficult hatch to fish with success due to the millions of naturals on the water at once. A slight twitch of your artificial as it drifts along will improve your chances.

The White Winged Black (*Tricorythodes*), number 20 or 22, is most prevalent in August. This hatch is called *Caenis* by some; the two genera are very similar. It brings up many fish, and good ones, to feed on it.

The last of the important mayflies is *Paraleptophlebia bicornuta*, the Slate Mahogany Dun, size 16, which is a September occurrence, with a morning hatch and an evening spinner fall.

There are several stone flies in Henry's Fork. *Pteronarcys californica*, the salmonfly, is the largest and most numerous. It populates boulder-filled fast-water stretches, Box and Cardiac canyons, and other such places. It commences to emerge in the waters below Mesa Falls in late May and usually reaches Box Canyon early to mid-June. This, if the weather cooperates, can be pandemonium time. I've seen several of these hatches smothered in six inches of wet snow. But the nymph is in the water three or four years and is always useful. Both nymph and dry are size 4, 3XL or 4XL. See Appendix B for a list of patterns for nymph and adult. A smaller yellow stone fly, *Doroneuria theodora*, about size 8, 2XL, hatches during and after the salmonfly. This is the Amber, or Yellow, Stone pattern in both nymph and adult.

The many caddis species hatch through the summer into fall. I've found that Elk Hair, Colorado King and Goddard Caddis patterns in sizes 12 through 18 will handle any of these.

The big streamers in the heavy fast water produce excellent catches of very large trout. I like the golden badger Spruce (called Dark Spruce) in size 2 to 2/0, Green or Brown Marabou Muddlers in the same sizes, a sculpin pattern or a size 2 Mickey Finn for anywhere in faster water.

The stream is full of leeches. I've only found brown ones, but fellows who haunt the stream tell me that olive ones are more numerous. So, for a possible trophy fish, have brown and olive leeches, Woolly Buggers or even Matukas, size 6, 3XL through 2.

One always wants to have the terrestrials with him. Ants, crickets, beetles and hoppers often perform magic to bring up big fish after your most slavish imitations have failed.

In spite of its being loaded with trout most places, the Henry's Fork is the most challenging trout stream I know. It is so loaded with trout food that the fish are not only choosy, there are times when I believe they are actually insolent. But the opportunity is huge, and the fish are, too.

Hayden Valley.

11
Yellowstone River

This stream was named by the Indians a century or more before the whites came into the area. It was first known of by white men in 1743 when La Verendrye reached the area of the Mandan Villages. David Thompson of the North West Company is credited with the first writing of the name in English, in 1798. But Thompson did not explore beyond the river's mouth on the Missouri.

It rises in two branches, the higher on the west slope of Yount's Peak (12,161 feet high) in the Shoshone Range of Wyoming. The Shoshone, Wind River and Absaroka ranges are all part of the same peak system that extends from Dubois, Wyoming, to Livingston, Montana.

The first tributaries, Thorofare and Atlantic creeks, join the stream on the Thorofare Plateau at about 8,000 feet. It first becomes a trout stream here, and for the next twenty-five river miles before entering Yellowstone Lake, elevation 7,733 feet, it is a meandering, many-channeled brook with a clean gravel or sand-silt bottom. It lies in a broad valley, one to three miles across, which is often marshy or boggy.

This area is as primitive and wild now as it was 200 years ago when it was one of the most difficult spots in the West to reach. It is still the most difficult, time-consuming place in Yellowstone Park to get to, and three days is about the minimum time required to visit and fish it. The fish are neither larger nor more plentiful than in the river below the lake. Still, if one wishes to fish an almost untouched trout stream in beautiful surroundings, there is probably none anywhere in the forty-eight lower states that have been less affected by man than this one.

From the lake, which collects the input of more than a score of icy streams, the river emerges as one of the largest trout streams in the nation, and one of the best.

The well-intentioned abuses of earlier years—trapping, stripping, restocking in an effort to help nature—have largely been stopped. The river is now left pretty much to nature, and is being managed for the welfare of the creatures in and around it with the result it has become perhaps as natural a trout stream as currently exists, outside of Alaska or remote Canada, on this continent.

The first mile below the outlet has been closed to fishing for about five years. This includes the famous Fishing Bridge, an atrocity in its time. From the end of this closed area to the start of the next at Sulphur Caldron, is little more than six miles of water so unbelievably good that it supports about 4,500 anglers per mile of stream during the season and still maintains its quality. It is catch-and-release fishing, perhaps the most prolific such piece of water anywhere in the world. It is possible to catch and release over seventy-five trout averaging two pounds in a day's fishing, and catches of fifty or more are not at all uncommon. It is currently restricted to flies and single-hook lures.

Just below the lake outlet, the river is broad, 300 to 400 feet across, and there are boggy areas that one must be aware of and watch out for. Only a small portion of the water can be covered by wading and flotation devices of any kind are banned. It holds an enormous pod of trout.

A little farther on the banks become better defined and road and river edge closer together. Two road miles below the outlet the two parallel each other in close proximity all through this splendid fishing stretch. Mostly the river is a large, deep, gliding stream over a clean gravel bottom. This picture is deceiving. This is a very powerful river, moving relentlessly to its downstream falls. One can stand in his waders out in the river and feel a steady movement of the gravel under his feet. In time one will be edged steadily and slowly downstream without volition.

Le Hardy Rapids is a beautiful fast-water stretch about halfway between the lake outlet and Sulphur Caldron. At times, for study and management purposes, it is closed to fishing.

Buffalo Ford is the well-known spot where anglers by the score gather. On some days, as many as 150 fishermen will visit this quarter-mile-long stretch and, incredibly, all will catch from a few to many trout, running one to three, and occasionally more, pounds.

This is a place where even a person in a wheelchair may catch fish. One can park on a nearly flat shore within fifty feet of the water's edge and the wheelchair can be rolled over and into the shallows. There is a spot where a cast of thirty or thirty-five feet will put the fly over one of the most productive channels. The handicapped can not only hook, but net their own fish here. And the handicapped spin fisher can cover a third or more of the river from a wheelchair. Nor is this the only place in the Park where this may be done. There are no more accessible trout waters anywhere in the world.

The Yellowstone River is an excellent place to bring children, or persons who have never fished, to introduce them to one of the most universal—and unexplainable—joys

Near Sulphur Caldron area.

LeHardy Rapids area.

that exists. It is also a place where it is easy to teach them the value of conservation and ecological protection because they can feel as well as see the results.

The section of the river below Sulphur Caldron down to Alum Creek, a little more than six miles of water, is a marshy, boggy area that is loaded with wildlife and waterfowl. It is closed to fishing as a nature study area, and it is a pure joy to visit. On any given day one may see buffalo, moose, deer, antelope, coyotes, muskrat and marmots, as well as birds and waterfowl—including the rare and beautiful trumpeter swan. The closing of this area for this purpose is another example of the Park Administration moving closer to the ideal in managing this wonderland for *all* creatures, and for the continued enjoyment by mankind.

Below Alum Creek to Chittenden Bridge over the river just above Upper Falls, the bottom is a rather featureless affair of various silts, muds and clays over rhyolite lava bedrock. This is less propitious water for trout and aquatic insects and the fish are fewer. However, there is reason to believe that trout migrate into and out of the area, for reasons presently unexplained, and one can occasionally hit a bonanza here. But venture no closer than a quarter-mile of the bridge. The current here is picking up speed for its leap over the falls, the bottom becomes smooth bedrock, and several unwary anglers have been swept to their death. This is a very powerful river here and elsewhere and must be treated with intelligence and respect.

The Grand Canyon of the Yellowstone is as beautiful and as awe inspiring as that of the Colorado. There are choice, safe locations from which it may be viewed. There are trout in the river throughout its length, but they are neither larger nor more plentiful than elsewhere. It is a minimum 1,500-foot vertical climb into and out of, and if it is solitude in angling that you are after, it may be had far easier in the Black Canyon, a mile or two below—downstream—of the mouth of the Grand Canyon.

The river comes out of the Grand Canyon in the vicinity of Tower Falls (on Tower Creek, a tributary). There is a mile or two of good, fast, boulder-filled pocket water up and down stream of the Cooke City Road Bridge that is great fun to fish if you like fast-water fishing. I like it.

Black Canyon stretches for about twenty miles from its head just below the bridge, all the way to Gardiner. From the head of the canyon to Gardiner, it is out of sight of, and from one to four miles from the Mammoth–Tower Junction Road. This is the longest uninterrupted stretch of the river, and for those who can make a relatively easy hike, it is the best place in the world to find solitude and good fishing at a rather small physical price.

The terrain is not difficult to cross in most areas. The ground cover is mostly sagebrush and bunchgrass, interspersed with common juniper. The footing is good, and it takes only from half to one and a half hours to reach the river from the road.

This is fast water, runs, rapids and cascades, even a falls. There are some giant smooth-surfaced pools, but they are pools with a powerful current. The pool bottoms are polished bedrock, the rest of the stream bottom is large rubble and boulders. Waders

In the Black Canyon of the Yellowstone.

Mud Volcano area.

cannot generally be used, so wear your hiking boots.

It is stone fly water and the nymphs live from one to four years in the stream before emerging as flying adults. There are several caddis species that generally are found along the current edges and in the quieter waters. The best fly most of the time is the big, weighted stone fly nymph, but here you will need more kinds and sizes than elsewhere. Both the black *Pteronarcys* and the golden amber *Calineuria, Doroneuria* and *Hesperoperla* are found in numbers. Salmonflies here include all three species, and you'll find them hatching in June, July, August and even into September. So, along with the nymphs and a sinking line, one wants to carry the dries and a floating line.

You will probably not see another angler except your own party along this stretch. It is fished only by the very dedicated. Yet it is not that difficult of access and is excellent fishing for strong, wild, lusty fish of one and two pounds.

In effect, it is an undisturbed, wilderness river, close to a major roadway, that offers solitude and superb fishing for the angler willing to walk a bit.

If I were going back into any of the stretches farthest from the road, I would take a sleeping bag, the necessary permits, several ready-to-eat meals, my fishing gear, and I'd spend the night. I would take a compass and a map, because once off the road the country looks much alike, and the river changes directions. You might not get lost, but you could hike several extra miles to gain your objective.

If you take the above precautions, you will have a most enjoyable angling experience and one that few people have taken. Also, while in there, you will get the feeling that this was what the world was like before man came upon the scene. It's worth making the trip just for that.

NATURALS AND ARTIFICIALS

In that section of the river above the Grand Canyon, the mayflies are *Ameletus, Callibaetis coloradensis* and perhaps one other species, *Drunella grandis;* the Western Green Drake; two species of *Ephemerella;* one *Heptagenia; Baetis; Epeorus longimannus,* Western Quill Gordon, and *Siphlonurus occidentalis,* the Gray Drake.

Thus one wants a black and gray nymph, sizes 12 and 10, for all but one of the mayfly nymphs. A Gold Ribbed Hare's Ear nymph, size 10, will do for *Ameletus.*

Caddis of all kinds, and there are many, may be handled with our old standby soft-hackle wets in sizes 10 through 16, with gray, brown, tan, yellow and green bodies. The caddis dries are covered by the Elk Hair, Colorado King and, increasingly, by the

Goddard patterns in 10, 12, 14, 16 and 18.

At times, in the no-kill section above Sulphur Caldron, you will find the fish feeding exclusively on the ridiculously small *Chironomid* (midge) larvae or the ridiculously large *Dytiscus* (riffle beetle) larvae. So, have a midge larval-pupal pattern in size 20, and either my Riffle Devil pattern, if you can find it, or a ginger-hackle, olive-bodied Woolly Worm in size 4, 4XL. Believe me, there will be times when one or the other is all that the fish will take.

The stone flies are *Pteronarcys californica* with its black nymph, *Pteronarcella badia*, also black, and the golden-amber nymphal types of *Calineuria californica, Doroneuria theodora, Hesperoperla pacifica* and three members of *Perla* and *Alloperla*. These all are similar in color, but vary greatly in size, from 12 regular to 4, 4XL. If you have either Amber, or Yellow, Stone patterns in those sizes, you're all set.

In general, if you refer to the Appendixes in the back, you will find the pattern you need to match any of the naturals you are likely to encounter. There may be times when you will be stumped by some strange insect for which I've listed neither scientific name nor artificial counterpart. If this happens, grab a specimen and come see me. I'll give you a cup of coffee or a cold beer, and we'll see what we can come up with.

Above Sulphur Caldron area.

LAST CAST

You will note that I've mentioned several different regulations in different places throughout this book, without pinning them down. Regulations in this area— Yellowstone Park, southwestern Montana and southeastern Idaho—are constantly undergoing changes as fish and wildlife people strive to produce and maintain quality fisheries. Help them help you to better fishing by obtaining and obeying the rules they work so hard to intelligently apply.

In releasing trout, do not sacrifice them on the altar of false sportsmanship. Use a strong enough leader so that you can land them while they are still full of life and have a better chance of living. Don't play them until they die of boredom. And use a net. You can net a trout with less harm than beaching or hand-grabbing it.

If a trout swallows your nymph, or other fly, cut the leader and let it go. You can tie another fly in a few minutes, or buy one for a dollar. It takes years to grow a good trout, and they are invaluable alive and in the stream. They are far too valuable to be caught only once, as the great Lee Wulff wisely observed over forty years ago.

Learn the manners and etiquette that have made our great sport one of the most civilized. Walk softly and away from the bank, well away when coming downstream. Never needlessly disturb the fish or another's fishing. The Golden Rule—do unto others as you would have them do unto you—was made by a fisherman. Keep it and abide by it.

In Yellowstone Park, no license to fish is required, but a free permit is. Upon signing it, you are attesting that you know, understand and will obey the regulations, will have the permit on your person and display it on request. Failure to do so can get you a trip to see the U.S. Commissioner and a heavy fine.

No true sportsman will litter or otherwise desecrate the lovely surroundings in which trout streams are invariably found. If you take it in, bring it out. Remember: While you may not want it, neither does anyone else.

I implore you not *ever* to discard coils or lengthy pieces of nylon monofilament. If you've ever seen fish, birds or animals entrapped in this vicious material, cut, choked, starving or dead, then you know what a terrible thing it is.

Forgive me these gentle remonstrations. But there are so many millions of us now that it requires constant attention on the part of all of us if our sport and the beauty of its environment are to survive.

Near Lewis River between Lewis Lake and Shoshone Lake.

Photographer's Notes

The genesis of this book came from a book published in 1938 titled *The Waters of Yellowstone with Rod and Fly*. It was written by Howard Back, a professor at the University of Houston who, like a lot of us, had fallen in love with Yellowstone Park and its rivers. His feelings were so strong that he wanted to share them. The book is lovely and Back's phrases are as lyrical as the Firehole River singing in the June sunshine. *The Waters of Yellowstone with Rod and Fly* has been out of print a long time. It's a collector's item, and hard to find. I am lucky enough to have a copy. I love to photograph Yellowstone as much as I love to fish there. And I liked Back's book so much that I went through his book and found descriptions of specific locations on Yellowstone's rivers. Then I began photographing the places. Then a second idea came to me. There was not a guidebook in print on fishing in Yellowstone, but there should be. I knew there was only one man to do the text, Charlie Brooks, the dean and the sage of the Yellowstone fishing writers. Charlie liked the idea, so now we have *Fishing Yellowstone Waters*.

I am hoping that some of the readers are photographers, or will be. Photography will add a new dimension to your love of rivers and fishing and to your life. You will see things you never saw before, sunshine and shadow will have much more meaning for you.

In taking the pictures for this book, I used both 35mm and 2¼ × 2¼ formats. My 35mm cameras are all Nikons—an FTN, a Nikkormat ELW, an F3, and a Nikonos IV-A. I have an auto-winder for the ELW and the F3 has a motor drive. The Nikon lenses used were a 24mm, 35mm, 50mm (normal), 55mm macro, 35-105mm zoom and a 80-200mm zoom. Additionally, I have a Novaflex Close-Up system with a 105mm lens and a Novaflex 400mm and 600mm follow focus lens system. You really don't need this much to start out, though. For someone who wants to take photographs of fishing and rivers I would recommend the following three lenses first: a zoom lens in the 35 105mm area, a 55mm macro for close-up work but which will also focus to infinity, and another zoom in the 80–200mm range, which provides you with a medium telephoto lens. Zoom lenses save you carrying a lot of other lenses on your river expeditions. Over the last few years their quality has improved remarkably—along with their numbers.

Buy the very best quality camera body that you can afford, and one, of course, that will accept interchangeable lenses. If you are serious now about photography, or think that you could become serious, plan ahead about what equipment you will get. This part you will find easy. Stay within the line of lenses and equipment that are made by the manufacturer of the camera you choose. After all, they planned them for your camera. I like Nikon because of its superb, high quality, its day-in day-out dependability, and because their tough, rugged equipment will stand up with a lot of hard use and, at the same time, maintain its precision. There are other fine camera systems too, including Canon, Leica, Pentax, and Minolta. Each makes a full line of cameras, lenses and equipment.

If there is one camera I would never be without, and if there is one camera I can recommend to you if you just want one to have with you while you are fishing, it would have to be the Nikonos. It is made by Nikon also and the present model is the IV-A. It is actually an underwater camera good to a depth of 160 feet. While I don't recommend trying to take pictures at this depth while you are fishing, I do strongly recommend this camera if you are only going to get one for use on the river (and in it) or if you want a camera with you all the time while you are fishing and you don't want to take the chance of falling in with your more expensive, nonwaterproof camera. I try to make it a rule to have the Nikonos around my neck all the time while I am fishing. If I break the rule something invariably happens that would have made a wonderful photograph. Last time it was a ten-pound steelhead that jumped three times about thirty feet in front of me.

The Nikonos IV-A has an automatic exposure system and you can interchange lenses. There is a short 80mm telephoto that is the most useful and I always carry one while I'm fishing. It is small and light and fits easily in my vest. There are several other waterproof cameras on the market that are good also. But I still like the Nikonos. It's built like a waterproof tank, it's dependable, it's fast enough, and the lens is good enough that you can make prints up to 16×20 from its negatives that are very fine indeed. I see them advertised (with the 35mm slightly wide-angle lens it comes with) for less than a good graphite fly rod. If you spend a lot of time on rivers it's worth it. If you buy one, get into the habit of having it around your neck. Pretty soon you won't even notice it's there. Later, you'll miss it if it isn't there. A camera of this type is a stream companion. One June afternoon last year on the Firehole a mother elk and her newborn calf came quietly down through the lodgepole pine to the bank opposite me. I went to my bank, put down my fly rod, and slowly crossed the river to be near them, but not so

Cutthroat Trout under water at Yellowstone River.

Mt. Haynes on the Upper Madison.

close that it would disturb them. Somehow, I think the mother knew I meant no harm.

My 2¼ × 2¼ is a Hasselblad. More accurately, it is a system. I use this when I have more time as it is not as fast or mobile as a 35mm single-lens reflex camera. It has interchangeable backs, making it possible to change types of film quickly. The Hasselblad has long been considered the state of the art in medium-format cameras. It is also the state of the art in price, but worth every penny. The Hasselblad system is a complete line with lenses, film backs, motor drives, viewing screens, filters, and every other type of accessory, all interchangeable. The negative (or slide) is almost five times as large as 35mm and has better sharpness, too. However, 35mm films have been improved so much recently that this difference has diminished considerably. Still, you will notice a distinct difference if you project a 2¼ × 2¼ slide and a 35mm slide. I use the Hasselblad when I have more time to set up and get organized and try to use it with a tripod as much as possible. By all means one should have a 35mm camera system first.

Carrying camera equipment along, in, or across a river is always a problem. Generally, where there is no danger of falling in, and for storage, I use backpacks rather than regular camera bags. On the river it is easier to have your hands free and the camera equipment on your back while going from one place to another. In October of 1982 Charlie Brooks, Craig Mathews (he and his wife, Jackie, have the Blue Ribbon Fly Shop in West Yellowstone) and I took a boat across Lewis Lake and walked about five miles up the Lewis Channel to the outlet at Shoshone Lake. The idea was for Charlie and Craig to fish and for me to take pictures. My backpack of cameras weighed about fifty pounds on the way in and about one hundred pounds on the way out. But I never would have been able to get the camera equipment in as easily without the backpack. There are many special backpacks (and vests), made specifically for cameras and camera equipment. When I am going to take a small amount of camera equipment across the river, or in a boat down the river, I use an inexpensive waterproof bag made by Sima. They come in two sizes and with shoulder straps; besides that they're inexpensive and they work. Sima calls them "Sports Pouches" and they're a good investment for fine equipment.

I use mainly Kodak film because I've gotten to know it and it's readily available. Always take more film than you need. When you consider everything, film is the most inexpensive item. If you are there and going to take photographs, do it and try to shoot several shots of the elk, in the quiet light of dusk on the Madison or your fishing buddy landing the big brown on the Firehole, and when you see a beautiful sunrise or sunset on a Yellowstone river, don't be afraid to use ten shots from different angles, and perspectives, and with different exposures. One of these may be the one that you will love. Bracket your shots for different exposures by changing the f stop or the shutter speed so that you shoot at least one shot over, and one shot under, what the camera says is the correct exposure. For color-slide film, I like Kodachrome 25 and Kodachrome 64 if there is enough light, and Ektachrome 400 if there isn't. The black-and-white photographs in this book were made from negatives from Kodak Panatomic X (ASA 32), Plus X (ASA 100) and Tri-X (ASA 400). Mainly, they are from Pan X and Tri-X film. If there

Near LeHardy Rapids.

was enough light or if I had time to put the camera on a tripod, I used the slower Pan X, which has finer resolution and better sharpness. Tri-X is a faster film, which means you can get a picture with less light. If you must settle on just one film, I recommend Tri-X.

There is a fairly new film on the market that appears to me to be an absolute boon to river and fishing photographers who like to shoot black and white. It is made by Agfa and called Vario-XL. You can expose this film from ASA 125 all the way to ASA 1600 and no compensation is necessary during development. In other words, it can be processed normally with nothing extra having to be done because of shooting the film at different film speeds. The prints from the negatives are surprisingly good. So you can shoot from the bright, flat light of noon into the dim light of dusk and not change film and usually have enough film speed to get photographs you otherwise would not.

Even a day trip along the river, or in a boat, presents a space problem. The problem becomes more acute if you carry film in your fishing vest. So I always take the film out of the box, but *leave* it in the plastic film can. I put a piece of adhesive tape across the film-can cap and write on it, with a waterproof marker, the type of film, number of exposures, and expiration date. For example—"TRI-X PAN 36, June 85." I use different color markers for different films.

Some of you develop your own film and know the joys of this. Hopefully, some of you will if you don't now. It will bring you untold fulfillment and bring your rivers to your darkroom. I thought you might be interested in how I develop my black-and-white negatives. Generally, my procedures are based on a 20-percent overdevelopment because I use what is called a "cold light" enlarger. I develop Panatomic X in Agfa Rodinal developer, diluted 100 to 1, for eighteen minutes. Plus X is developed also in Agfa Rodinal developer, diluted 75:1, for 14½ minutes. The old standby, Tri-X, is developed in Kodak HC 110 B, 1 ounce plus enough water to make the whole 32 ounces, for 9½ minutes.

When shooting color I almost always try to use a polarizer to get more color saturation and to bring out the clouds. When shooting black and white I often use an orange filter, less often a yellow filter. I like the effects an orange filter has on a black-and-white film. It will bring out clouds dramatically, improve the contrast in landscapes, and darken blue water. A yellow filter will darken a blue sky to a more natural rendition and bring out the clouds. For very dramatic skies and clouds, try a red filter. A green filter will lighten green foliage and trees and render good skin tones. Filters are relatively inexpensive for 35mm cameras and screw right into the top of your lens. I even carry a few filters with me in my fishing vest to use on the Nikonos. A word of caution about the use of filters in Yellowstone: you will be, in the Park, anywhere from 6,000 to 10,000 feet above sea level. The skies aren't always blue in Yellowstone but when they are, at these elevations, there can be an excess of blue light. This excess can have a pronounced effect on black-and-white film when a filter is used. As an example, at this altitude a yellow filter can sometimes have the dramatic effects a red filter would have near sea level.

One camera accessory I would absolutely recommend that you have in Yellowstone is a simple bean bag. Mine was made by my wife out of a tough nylon fabric available in most material shops. It is about nine inches long and 3½ inches in diameter. She put a slit in the middle with a Velcro closure, so the beans can be put in and taken out. That bean bag, with a camera on it, has been on a lot of rocks and next to a lot of trees in Yellowstone. It is a quick, sturdy camera support. You don't always have time for the tripod. Some of the greatest photographic opportunities in Yellowstone are right from your car while you are driving slowly along a river. The animals are there, so are the fishermen, and so the good light can be too. You can get the bean bag on the door, with the window down, and your camera on top of it, quickly and easily, and not miss a wonderful scene that might be there just for a moment. In the car, or on the river, you will find that you must be very quick with the camera at times.

Here are some other suggestions that may help you in taking photographs in Yellowstone, or anywhere else for that matter. 1. *Support.* Get as stable as you can. Use your tripod if time permits, otherwise a bean bag for support. Put your camera, and the bean bag if you have it, on the car door, a rock, the car hood or a branch. Otherwise, if you can, lie down or sit down. Tighten the camera to yourself by stretching the strap against you. Inhale as you are about to shoot and squeeze the shutter release. 2. *Telephoto lens.* Always use a shutter speed that equals or exceeds the focal length of the lens; i.e., if using a 200mm telephoto lens use a shutter speed of ½₂₅₀ faster. 3. *Simplicity.* Exclude all extraneous or unnecessary matter from your picture. This can include using a low f stop to reduce your depth of field. 4. *Camera itself.* Learn it thoroughly, and the instruction book that comes with it. The camera controls should become second nature. 5. *Composition.* Remember that the subject does not always have to be in the center of the picture. Try putting it to either side. Don't take all your photographs with the camera in a horizontal position. Turn it, and take some with the camera in a vertical position. Move up and down with the camera. Change the perspective. 6. *Exposure.* Expose color film for the highlight areas and black-and-white film for the shadow areas in which you want detail. Bracket your shots. 7. *Wildlife.* Remember that the animals in Yellowstone are wild. So even though they may appear tame because they are protected and somewhat used to man, treat them with the respect they deserve. This means that you should keep your distance, even though everyone else appears to be descending on the poor animal, and try to use telephoto lenses. With patience you will find many opportunities for wildlife photographs in Yellowstone with the animals in their natural surroundings, without people and automobiles around them. Remember that Yellowstone is managed, as it should be, for its wildlife and natural resources. You and I are just visitors. 8. *Time of day.* If you want to see the park at its best, and have the best photographic opportunities, go out early, very early, even before the sun is up, and go out late, and stay until it is dark. The wildlife is out then, the people aren't. I can't emphasize this enough. 9. *Places.* I wish space permitted me to tell you all the places to be sure to go. But maybe it's best that you find them yourself. A few suggestions: drive slowly along the rivers, early and late; include the Lamar Valley and Hayden Valley in your explorations; get out and walk. Yellowstone is full of trails, short and long, well marked and mapped. A friend and I spent four days backpacking in the Black Canyon of the Yellowstone a few years ago and we didn't see anyone else the whole time. Two and one-half million people visit Yellowstone annually now. Few leave the road.

Most of the superior photographers I know are generous, warm people. Ralph Wahl's great black-and-white photographs of Northwest steelhead rivers caused me to take up photography seriously. There is not, in my opinion, a finer set of black-and-white photographs than those in Wahl's book *Come Wade the River,* which he put together with excerpts from Rod Haig-Brown's books. I got to know Ralph Wahl after seeing his photographs and he spent a lot of time teaching me his developing systems for black and white and how to mount and mat photographs. Lefty Kreh and I spent a day in the park together several years ago. He drove the car and talked to me about photography while I took notes. I still have the notes. Lefty, besides being another great photographer, truly has the gift of teaching. So maybe the second most important thing I can tell you about Yellowstone (the first will follow) is to stop and talk to the numerous serious photographers there. Don't bother them if they are in the middle of photographing the trumpeter swans at Seven Mile Bridge on the Madison. Wait for the opportune time. I am always amazed at how much can be learned this way and how much enjoyment one gets from giving a few suggestions to others.

I owe a lot to my friend Jack Hemingway, who first introduced me to Yellowstone and taught me most of what I know about fly fishing for trout. My friends Ernie Schwiebert, Craig Mathews, and Jim Nelson (The Phantom) have all been very patient and kind to let me take photographs while they were fishing. It was a rare pleasure to work with Charlie Brooks. His enthusiasm and energy are boundless. I could hardly keep up with him. He is a great researcher. His knowledge of Yellowstone is intimate, his love deep.

This is supposed to be a guide book to fishing the finest trout fishing waters in the continental United States. The most important thing I can tell you is that there is more in Yellowstone than just fishing if one will stop, and look, and sense and feel. I think Howard Back expressed it best in *The Waters of Yellowstone with Rod and Fly* when he said:

> I have explained, then, how in a sense this work is a guide-book to the principal angling waters of Yellowstone. That is true, and yet it is more than a guide-book in its literal sense. You will find in it something of the imagination as well, for facts without fancy are but dull affairs. You will find a little of the hills and dales, of the flowers and the birds and the wild things, of the romance that lies deep in all of us, disguise it how we will. For is it not of all these things that the true meaning of that wonder word "angling" is made up?

I hope that you find some of those things in this book too. Most of all, I hope it helps you to discover and love Yellowstone.

DAN CALLAGHAN
In Cabin 1 At Steamboat Inn
On The North Umpqua River
October 27, 1983

Green Drake on Railroad Ranch.

Appendixes

APPENDIX A

Insects of the Area and Some Artificials to Represent Them

MONTH OF EMERGENCE	SCIENTIFIC NAME	ARTIFICIAL FLY OR COMMON NAME	HOOK SIZE
Mayflies			
April–October	*Baetis* spp.	Blue Dun Blue Winged Olive	14-22
Mid-June–Late September	*Callibaetis nigritis* *Callibaetis coloradensis*	Speckled Dun Speckled Spinner	14-22
September–October	*Centroptilum* spp.	White Winged Sulphur Drake	20
25 June–20 August	*Drunella flavlinea*	Slate Winged Olive	14
Mid-June–Mid-July	*Drunella grandis*	Western Green Drake	10

MONTH OF EMERGENCE	SCIENTIFIC NAME	ARTIFICIAL FLY OR COMMON NAME	HOOK SIZE
5 July–Mid-August	*Epeorus albertae*	Blue Winged Salmon Dun	14
Mid-June–Mid-July	*Epeorus longimanus*	Western Quill Gordon	14
1 June–Mid-July	*Epeorus nitidus*	Slate Winged Maroon Drake	14
May–July	*Ephemerella lacustris* *Ephemerella inermis* *Ephemerella infrequens*	Pale Morning Dun	16
June–Mid-July	*Ephemera simulans*	Brown Drake	10-12
Late June–Mid-July	*Isonychia velma*	Western Leadwing	10
September–Mid-July	*Paraleptophlebia bicornuta*	Mahogany Dun	16
Mid-July–Mid-October	*Pseudocloeon* spp.	Tiny Blue Winged Olive	22
August–October	*Siphlonurus occidentalis*	Gray Drake	10
July–September	*Tricorythodes* spp.	White Winged Black	20

Caddis

May–October	*Brachycentrus* spp.	Colorado King Little Grey Caddis (pupa)	14, 16, 18

| September | *Dicosmoecus atripes* | Bucktail Caddis
Great Orange Sedge | 8, 2XL |
| May–October | *Rhyacophila* spp. | Elk Hair Caddis
Little Green Caddis
  (pupa) | 14, 16, 18 |

Stone Flies

| Hatch not important | *Calineuria californica*
Doroneuria theodora
Hesperoperla pacifica | Yellow Stone (nymph)
Amber Stone (nymph)
Brown Stone
Willow Fly Nymphs | 6, 3XL
8, 3XL
8, 2XL |
| June–July | *Pteronarcys californica* | Bird's Stonefly
Sofa Pillow
  and many more dry
  patterns | 4, 3XL |

See Appendix B for nymph patterns of P. californica.

Dragon-Damsel Flies

Adult not important. Use nymphs of tan or brown, size 8, 2XL to 4, 2XL for dragon nymph (weighted). Use tan, brown or green damsel nymphs, sizes 6, 8 and 10, all 2XL. Use weighted or unweighted.

Our rivers cover hundreds of miles, 3,000 feet difference in elevation and vary greatly in temperature. All emergence (hatch) times are approximate and will vary by stream.

APPENDIX B

Most Used Fly Patterns and Sizes

FLY TYPE	PATTERN	SIZE
Dragon & Damsel Nymphs	Assam Dragon (Charlie Brooks' pattern)	4, 2XL
	Randall's Dragon	6, 2XL
	Fair Damsel, Green Damsel, Dave's Damsel	8, 2XL
Mayfly Dry	Adams	10, 12, 14, 16
	Blue Dun, Blue Winged Olive	16, 18
	Brown Drake	10
	Light Cahill	14, 16
	Pale Morning Dun	16
	Slate Winged Maroon Drake	12, 14
	Slate Winged Olive	14,16
	Speckled Spinner and Dun	14, 16
	Tup's Indispensable	14, 16
	Western Green Drake	10
	Western Quill Gordon (Brown Dun)	12, 14
	White Winged Black	20
	White Winged Sulphur Drake	20, 22
Caddis Dry	Colorado King	12-18
	Elk Hair Caddis, Goddard Caddis	10-18
	Henryville Special, Kings River Caddis	12-16
	Bucktail Caddis (yellow and orange bodies)	6, 8, 10, 12
	Great Orange Sedge	8, 2XL
Stone Fly Dry (Salmonflies)	Bird's Stonefly	4, 3XL
	Bucktail Caddis (yellow and orange bodies)	6, 3XL
	Doug's Super Stone	4, 3XL
	Henry's Fork Salmon	4, 3XL
	Parks' Salmon Fly	4, 3XL
	Troth's Salmon Fly	4, 3XL
	Salmon Hopper	4, 3XL
	(There are several other patterns of this salmonfly.)	

General Dry Flies	Ant patterns	12, 14, 16
	Dave's Hopper	6, 8, 3XL
	Henry's Fork Hopper	8, 10, 3XL
	Goofus Bug	10, 12, 14, 16
	Grey Fox Variant	10, 12
	Grey Wulff	10, 12
	Hair Wing Variant (House and Lot)	10, 12
	Joe's Hopper	8, 3XL
	Letort Hopper	10, 12, 14, 2XL
	Renegade	10, 12
	Royal Wulff	10–16
Stone Fly Nymphs	Bitch Creek	All 6, 3XL or
	Black Nature nymph	4, 4XL
	Box Canyon Stone	
	Buffalo Stone	
	Girdle Bug	
	Kaufmann's Stone	
	Montana Nymph	
	Montana Stone (Charlie Brooks' pattern)	
	Soufal	
	Troth's Terrible Stone	
	Woolly Worm (Black)	

(The above are only *some* of the patterns made to represent *Pteronarcys californica*, the black nymph.)

	Amber Stone	8, 2XL to 4, 3XL
	Golden Stone	8, 2XL to 6, 3XL
	Yellow Stone (Charlie Brooks' pattern)	4, 3XL

(These represent *Acroneuria, Calineuria, Doroneuria, Perla* and *Isoperla* stone fly nymphs.)

General Nymphs	Martinez Black	10, 12, 14
	Ida May (Charlie Brooks' pattern)	10, 12
	Pheasant Tail	8, 10, 12, 14, 16
	Gray Nymph	8, 10
	Beaver Pelt	6, 8
	Mossback	4, 6
	Fledermaus	4, 6, 8
	Thunderbug	6, 8, 2XL
	Otter Shrimp (Trueblood)	8, 10, 12
	Tellico Nymph	10, 12, 14
	Gold Ribbed Hare's Ear	10, 12, 14

Mormon Girl.

Rabbit Sculpin (left), Muddler Minnow (right).

Sofa Pillow.

Gold Ribbed Hare's Ear.

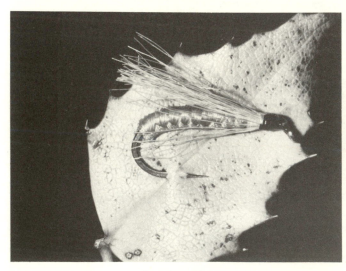

Sandy Mite.

Donelly Variant.

Montana Stone Nymph.

Goofus Bug (left), Hopper (right).

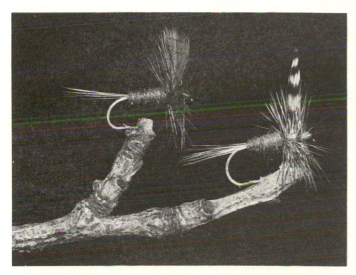

Blue Winged Olive (left), Adams (right).

Trude.

Vint's Special (left), Woolly Worm (right).

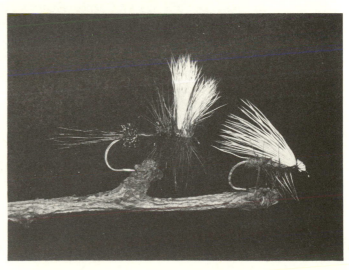

Royal Wulff (left), Elk Hair Caddis (right).

FLY TYPE	PATTERN	SIZE
General Wet Flies	Partridge—and Grouse-hackle flies with gray, green, orange, yellow and brown bodies	8, 10, 12, 14
	Brown Hackle, peacock	10, 12
	Carey Special	4, 6, 8, 10
	Grey Hackle, yellow and peacock	10, 12
	Blue Dun	12, 14
	Mallard Quill	14, 16
	Woolly Worm with yellow, brown and olive bodies	8, 3XL to 4, 4XL
	(Nearly all of the above patterns may be found in area shops, although *no* shop will carry them all.)	
Streamers and Such	Spruce, Light and Dark	2–2/0
	Muddler	2–2/0
	Brown Marabou Muddler	2–2/0
	Green Marabou Muddler	2–2/0
	Leech	2–2/0
	Woolly Bugger	2–2/0
	Vint's Special (Trude Streamer)	4, 4XL
	Matuka; Olive, Gray and Brown	2, 2XL
	Sculpin (Dave Whitlock's is best pattern)	2–2/0
	(Most shops carry the above flies in quantity.)	

In order to get the above information, Dan and I polled five shops in West Yellowstone, one in Ennis, and one in Last Chance (Henry's Fork). I also devised a rating system for the top ten most-used flies in the area from the information furnished by the shops. Each fly appearing as first choice on a list was rated ten points, a fly appearing second got nine, and so on down the list with the tenth fly receiving one point. Then all scores were totaled and the fly with the highest score appears as number one on the list below, and so on in order of diminishing totals.

1. Elk Hair Caddis   14
2. Royal Wulff   10
3. Hopper patterns   8–3X
4. Adams   12
5. Blue-wing Olive   16, Muddler Minnow   6 (tie)
6. Rabbit Sculpin   4, Gold-ribbed Hare's Ear   12, Montana Stone Nymph 4–4XL (tie)

7. Goofus Bug   10 and 12 (This fly was originated by a friend of Alexander MacDonald in 1938 or 1939 and developed and promoted into prominence by Pat and Sig Barnes of West Yellowstone. For many years Sig Barnes was the only professional tier tying the Goofus Bug.)

APPENDIX C

Historical Flies of the Yellowstone Area

The Trude, which began as a fat-bodied, hair-winged wet fly, was originated by Carter Harrison in 1903 while staying at Trude's Algenia Ranch on Henry's Fork. Vint Johnson, owner of the first fly shop in West Yellowstone, (1936) made the fly as a streamer called Vint's Special. It is very successful. Later, a visitor developed the Sofa Pillow (1948) as a dry version of the "salmon" fly for his wife, a beginning fly fisher, and Pat and Sig Barnes developed this fly as the only dry salmonfly pattern then available.

In the 1920s Franz Potts of Missoula developed the Mite patterns which became very popular in the Yellowstone area. They are still used with success. George Grant developed his series of nymphs from the tying methods of Potts.

The Woolly Worm was created in England about 1500 as a caterpillar imitation. It was used in the Missouri Ozarks in the 1920s as a bass fly. Don Martinez introduced it as a trout fly in West Yellowstone about 1936.

In 1936, Dan Bailey originated the Grizzly Wulff on the lower Madison and named it for his old friend, Lee Wulff.

The Martinez Black nymph was originated by Don Martinez of West Yellowstone about 1936. It is still as good a nymph pattern as any where a black nymph is needed.

The Mossback was developed by Dan Bailey about 1940 as a salmonfly nymph. It was also called Devil Scratcher.

Three flies were introduced into the West Yellowstone area in the early-to-mid 1940s by persons presently unknown. They still work. These are Mormon Girl, Montana Nymph, and Girdle Bug.

Roy Donnelly originated his series of large, bushy variants for the fast waters of the Madison Canyon and Snake River in Jackson's Hole circa 1942–44.

The Bitch Creek Nymph appeared about 1946 and has caused some controversy. There are streams called Bitch Creek in Southeast Idaho and near Helena, Montana, and people in those areas claim the fly. Also, in the 1950–65 period, a firm called Bitch Creek Flies claimed the pattern, but no one seems to know who actually originated this fly.

Jack Boehme of Missoula was a prolific originator of fly patterns. His Picket Pin, 1943, is a type, rather than a pattern and is named for the ground squirrel, the tail of which furnishes the hair for the wing of the fly.

All these flies are still used with success in the Yellowstone Waters area, and all of them have spawned imitations.

The Lower Madison near Cliff-Wade Lakes Bridge.

Bibliography

Back, Howard. The Waters of Yellowstone with Rod and Fly. New York: Dodd, Mead and Co., 1938.

Bergman, Ray. With Fly, Plug and Bait. New York: William Morrow and Co., 1947.

Brooks, Charles E., Larger Trout for the Western Fly Fisherman. New York: Nick Lyons Books/Winchester 1983.

_____. The Trout and The Stream. New York: Nick Lyons Books/Winchester 1974.

MacDonald, Alexander. Design for Angling. Boston: Houghton Mifflin Co., 1947.

_____. On Becoming a Fly Fisherman. New York: David Mc Kay Co., 1959.

Roemhild, G., Aquatic Insects of Yellowstone. Mammoth: The Yellowstone Institute, 1983.

Swisher, Doug, and Carl Richards, Selective Trout. New York: Nick Lyons Books/Winchester, 1971, 1983.

Varley, John D., and Paul Schullery. Freshwater Wilderness. Mammoth: The Yellowstone Library and Museum Association, 1983.

Index

Numbers in italics indicate illustrations.

Absaroka Range, 10, 28, 35, *36*, 123
Accomodations, 13–16
Adams fly, 24, 33, 41, 50, 66, *151*
Alum Creek (Yellowstone River), 127
Amber Stone fly, 41, 121, 131
Anderegg, Gene, 79
Antelope, 110, 127
Arch Rock (Merced River), 40
Assam Dragon fly, 32, 65
Atlantic Creek, 123

Back, Howard, 27, 135, 143
Bacon Rind Creek, 99
Bailey's Damsel fly, 32
Baker's Hole (Madison River), 16, *86*, 87, *89*, 97
Beartooth Range, 10, 27, 28
Beaver Meadows (Madison River), 87, 97
Beaverpelt (town), 32
Bergman, Ray, 59, 65, 69
Big Bend (Madison River), *78*, 79, 90, 97
Big Springs (Henry's Fork), 110–112
Bird's Stonefly fly, 24, 41, *92*
Biscuit Basin (Firehole River), 53, 56, *57*, 59, 64
Biscuit Basin Meadows (Firehole River), 59
Bitch Creek fly, 24
Black and Red Ant fly, 50
Black Canyon (Yellowstone River), 28, 127, *128*, 130, 143
Black Woolly Worm fly, 40, 41, 87
Blue Dun fly, 24, 33, 41, 66, 75, 97, 120
Blue Ribbon Fly Shop (West Yellowstone), 139
Blue Winged Olive fly, 33, 41, 50, 66, 75, 97, 120, 121, *151*
Box Canyon (Henry's Fork), *frontispiece*, 16, 112–113, *114*, 116, 120, 121
Bozeman (town), 107
Bridger, Jim, 56
Broads, the (Firehole River), 59, 65
Brooks, Charles, *95*, 135, 139, 143
Brook trout, 56, 112
Brown Bivisible fly, 51
Brown Drake fly, 120
Brown Marabou Muddler, 50, 87, 97, 121
Brown trout, *vi*, 46–49, 50, 56, 79
Bucktail Caddis fly, 41, 97
Buffalo, 127
Buffalo Ford (Yellowstone River), 124
Buffalo River, 16, 113
Bunsen Peak, 22

Cable Car Run (Madison River), 87
Callaghan, Dan, 28
Camera backpacks, 139
Cameras, 135–136, 139
Camera supports, 142
Cameron (town), 16
Canyon (town), 16
Cardiac Canyon (Henry's Fork), 110, 121
Carey Special fly, 25
Carmichael, Bob, 56–59
Carmichael's Fly Shop (Moose), 56
Channels, the (Madison River), 94
Chittenden Bridge (Yellowstone River), 127
Cliff-Wade Lake Bridge (Madison River), 90
Coachman fly, 25
Cold Mountain Creek, 43
Colorado King fly, 24, 33, 41, 50, 66, 75, 97, 104, 107, 121, 130
Come Wade the River (Wahl), 143
Connett, Gene, 101
Cooke City, 16, 27
Cooke City Road Bridge (Yellowstone River), 127
Coyotes, 127
Curlews, 110
Cutthroat trout, 31–32, 37, *39*, 101, 112, *137*

Dark Spruce Marabou Muddler fly, 97, 113
Dave's Hopper fly, 32
Deer, 127
Deerhair Mouse fly, 51, 66
De Lacy Creek, 43
Divide Creek, 99
Donelly Variant fly, *150*

East Gallatin River, 107
Elk, *52*, 70, 104, 137
Elk Hair Caddis fly, 24, 33, 41, 50, 66, 75, 87, 97, 104, 107, 121, 130, *151*
Elk Park (Gibbon River), 70, *73*
Ennis (town) 13, 16, 87, 94
Ennis Lake, 94
Excelsior Spring, 64

Fair Damsel fly, 32
Fan Wing Royal Coachman fly, 40
Fawn Creek, 19, 99
Film, 139–141
Film processing, 141
Filters, 142
Firehole Canyon, 56, 65, 70, 77

Firehole Falls, 56
Firehole River, *vi*, 9, 16, *58, 60, 61*, 70,
  75, 77, *78*
  Biscuit Basin section of, 56–59
  insect life on, 59, 64–65, 66
  recommended flies for, 65, 66–67
  smooth-water sections of, 59, 64–65
  temperature changes in, 53–56, 65–66
First Meadow (Slough Creek), 28, *30*,
  31–32
Fishing Bridge (Yellowstone River), 16,
  124
Fishless Days, Angling Nights (Sparse
  Grey Hackle), 120
Flick, Art, 81
Fly patterns, 17, 145–147, 148–149,
  150–151, 152–153
  historical, 153
Fountain Flats (Firehole River), 64–65
Freezeout Hole, 19

Gallatin Canyon, 101, 104–106
Gallatin Gateway (Gallatin River), 99,
  106
Gallatin Lake, 99
Gallatin Range, 10
Gallatin River, 9, 10, 12–16, *98*, 99, *100*,
  109
  canyon section of, 101, 104–106
  flat section of, 106
  insect life on, 104, 107
  recommended flies for, 101, 102, 106,
    107
  temperature of, 101
  upper section of, *102, 105*
  wading in, 99, 104
  Westfork area of, *103*
Gardiner (town), 16, 41
Gardner River, 9, 16, 19–24
  insect life on, 24
  recommended flies for, 24–25
  spawning run on, 24
  wildlife on, 19–22
Gardner's Hole (Gardner River), 16, 19
Gartside's Pheasant Hopper fly, 32
Gibbon Falls (Gibbon River), 70, 72, *74*
Gibbon Meadows (Gibbon River), 70, *71*
Gibbon River, 9, 65, 69, 77, *78*
  insect life on, 75
  recommended flies for, 70, 75
  sections of, 69–70
  upper, 16
Goddard Caddis fly, 24, 107, 121, 131
Godfrey, Will, *111*
Gold Ribbed Hare's Ear fly, 33, 40, 65,
  107, 130, *150*
Golden Olive Spinner fly, 41
Golden Stone fly, 41
Goofus Bug fly, 24, 33, 50, 75, 97, 104,
  151
Goose Lake Meadows (Firehole River),
  59, 64

Upper, *55, 63*
Grand Canyon (Yellowstone Park), 127,
  130
Granite Peak, 28
Grant Village, 16
Grasshopper Bank (Madison River), 81,
  82, 85
Grasshopper Glacier, 27
Gray Drake fly, 97, 130
Gray Nymph fly, 33, 65, 66, 97
Great Orange Sedge fly, 81, 97
Grebe Lake, 69
Greek Creek, 104
Green Damsel fly, 32
Green drake mayfly, *144*
Green Marabou Muddler, 50, 87, 97, 121
Grey Bivisible fly, 51
Grey Fox Variant fly, 33, 66, 70, 107
Grey Hackle fly, 25
Grey Wulff fly, 97
Grouse and Green fly, 25, 33
Grouse and Grey fly, 33
Grouse and Yellow fly, 33
Guides, 94

Haig-Brown, Rod, 143
Hair Wing Variant fly, 24, 50, 66, 70, 75
Hair Wing Variant (House and Lot) fly,
  33, 97
Hare's Ear fly, 41, 49, 50
Harriman State Park. *See* Railroad Ranch
Harrop, Rene, *118*
Harvey, George, 106
Hasselblad cameras, 139
Hayden Valley (Yellowstone River), 28,
  122, 143
Hebgen Dam (Madison River), 87
Hebgen Lake, 87
  resort area of, 16
Hemingway, Jack, *60*, 143
Hendrickson fly, 41, 50
Henry, Andrew, 109
Henry's Fork (Snake River), *frontispiece*,
  9, 10, 13, 16, 109
  Big Springs section of, 110–112
  Box Canyon section of, 112–116
  Henry's Lake Flat section of, 109,
    110–111
  insect life on, 112, 116, 120–121
  meadow section of, 110
  Pinehaven section of, 120
  Railroad Ranch section of, *115*, 116,
    117, 118, 119
  recommended flies for, 112, 113,
    120–121
  wading in, 113
  wildlife on, 110, 112
Henry's Lake, 9, 16, 109
Henry's Lake Flat (Henry's Fork), 109,
  110–111
Henry's Lake Range, 10
Herons, *83*, 110

Hewitt, Edward, 56
Hi-D sinking line, 87
Hole Number One (Madison River), 81
Hole Number Three (Madison River), 81
Hole Number Two (Madison River), 81
Holmes, Bob, 116
Hoodoo Basin (Lamar River), 35
Hoodoo Peak, 35
Hopper fly, *151*
Humboldt's Hole, 19

Ida May fly, 70, 97, 107
Indian Creek, 19
Iron Spring Creek, 53–54
Island Meadows (Madison River), 76, *80*
Island Park Caldera, 109
Island Park Dam (Henry's Fork), 16, 112
Island Park Lodge (Henry's Fork), 110
Island Park Village, 16
Island Park Summer Home area (Henry's Fork), 110

Jacklin, Bob, 113
Jacklin's Fly Shop (West Yellowstone), 32
Jackson's Hole, 19, 56
Jefferson River, 101, 109
Joe's Hopper fly, 32, 41
Johnson, Joe, 79
Joseph Peak, 19
Journal of a Trapper (1834–1843) (Russell), 28
Junction Pool (Lamar River), 35, 37

Karst, Don, *98*, 103
Karst's Ranch (Gallatin River), 16, 104
Kaufmann's Lake Dragon fly, 32
Keppler Cascades (Firehole River), 56
Kreh, Lefty, 143

La Branche, George, 51
Lake (town), 16
Lake trout, 46–49
Lamar River, 9, 16, 27, 28, 35, *36*, 37, *39*
    canyon section of, 37–40
    insect life on, 41
    meadow section of, 37
    recommended flies for, 40, 41
Lamar Valley (Yellowstone Park), 27, *34*, 35, 37, 38, 143
Langford-Washburn-Doane expedition, 77, 79
Last Chance (Henry's Fork), 16, 113, *115*, 116, *117*, *118*
Last Chance Run (Henry's Fork), 116
Lava Creek, 22
Leader tippets, 59
Le Hardy Rapids (Yellowstone River), 124, *126*, *140*

Lemke, Bing, *117*
Lenses, 136, 142
Lewis Canyon, *42*, 43
Lewis Channel, 139
Lewis Lake, 16, 43, 49, 50, 139
Lewis Lake Campground, 46
Lewis River, 9, 16, *134*
    above-the-falls section of, 46–49
    Channel section of, *45*, *48*, 49–50
    insect life on, 49, 50
    meadow stream section of, 43–46
    recommended flies for, 46, 49, 50–51
Lewis River Falls, *44*, *47*
Light Cahill fly, 24, 33, 41, 107
Lilly, Bud, 40
Little Firehole River, 53, 54
Long Riffle (Madison River), 81, *83*
Lower Coffee Pot rapids (Henry's Fork), 110
Lower Inn Bridge (Firehole River), 64

Mackinaw trout, *47*
Mack's Inn (Henry's Fork), 16, 110, 112
Madison Junction (Firehole River), 16, 65, 77, 79
Madison Junction Campground, 16
Madison Lake, 53
Madison Plateau, 79, *84*
Madison Range, 10
Madison River, 9, 10, 13, 16, 65, 70, 75, 77, 101, 109
    Baker's Hole section of, *86*, 87, *89*, 97
    Beaver Meadows section of, 97
    Big Bend section of, 79, 90, 97
    Channels section of, 94
    Grasshopper Bank section of, 81, *82*, *85*
    Hebgen Dam section of, 87–90
    insect life on, 79–81, 87, 97
    Long Riffle section of, 81, *83*
    lower, *88*, *91*, *92*, *93*, *95*, *154*
    meadows sections of, 77–79
    Nine Mile Hole section of, 79–81
    numbered holes sections of, 81, 87
    recommended flies for, 79, 81, 87, 90, 94, 97
    Seven Mile Run section of, 81
    Slide Inn Run section of, 90, *96*
    upper, *78*
Mammoth (town), 16, 22, *23*
Mandan Villages (Yellowstone River), 123
Marmots, *21*, 127
Marabou Muddler fly, 97, 113
Martinez Black fly, 33, 70, 97, 107
Mason, Bill, *114*
Mathews, Craig, *viii*, *26*, *115*, 139, 143
Mathews, Jackie, 139
Matukas fly, 121
Mayfly, 67
McAtee Bridge (Madison River), 90

McIntyre, Rich, 106
McRae's Bridge (Henry's Fork), 110
Merced River, 40
Mesa Falls (Henry's Fork), 110, *111*, 121
Metz, Bucky, 106
Mickey Finn fly, 121
Midway Geyser Basin (Firehole River), 64
Milepost 45 (Gallatin River), 107
Milepost 49 (Gallatin River), 101, 104
Milepost 22 (Gallatin River), 99, 101, 107
Missouri River, 109, 123
Montana Stone Nymph fly, 24, *151*
Moose, 104, 110, 127
Moose (town), 56
Moose Creek, 43
Mormon Girl fly, *150*
Morning Glory Pool (Firehole River), 53
Mount Haynes (Madison River), *138*
Mountain sheep, 104
Muddler Minnow fly, *151*
Mud Volcano (Yellowstone River), *129*
Muleshoe Bend (Firehold River), 54, 59, 64, 65, *67*
Muskrats, 127

National Park Meadows (Madison River), 70, 77, 97
National Park Mountain, *78*, 79
Nelson, Jim, *93*, 143
Nemes, Sylvester, 87
Nets, 17, 31
Nez Perce River, 65
Nikon cameras, 135–136
Nikonos IV-A camera, 136
Nine Mile Hole (Madison River), 79–81
Norris Geyser Basin (Gibbon River), 70
Norris Junction (Gibbon River), 77
Norris Meadows (Gibbon River), 69–70

Obsidian Creek, *18*, 19
Ojo Caliente Bend (Firehole River), 59, 64
Old Faithful geyser, 53, 56, 77
Old Faithful Inn and Lodge (Firehole River), 16
Olive Matuka fly, 97, 107
Osborne Bridge (Henry's Fork), 116, 120
Osprey Falls (Gardner River), 22, 24

Pale Morning Dun fly, 41, 50, 97, 121
Palisades Creek, 90
Panther Creek, 19
Parks' Fly Shop (Gardiner), 41
Parks, Richard, 41
Parks' Salmon Fly, 24–25
Parks' Stonefly, 41
Partridge and Orange fly, 25, 33
Peterson Palmer fly, 112

Pinehaven (Gallatin River), *12*, *98*
Pinehaven (Henry's Fork), 120
Pond's Lodge (Henry's Fork), 16, 112

Quake Lake, 87, 90
Quake Lake Slide, 109
Quill Gordon fly, 50

Rabbit Sculpin fly, *151*
Railroad Ranch (Henry's Fork), 16, *108*, 116, *119*
Rainbow trout, 101, *108*, 110, 112, *119*
Raynolds Pass, 109
Raynold's Pass Bridge (Madison River), *92*
Reed, Ann, 90
Reed, John, 90
Renegade fly, 33, 50, 75, 97
Riffle Devil fly, 131
Riverside Campground, 9, 13, 16, 120
Rocky Mountains, 10
Royal Wulff fly, 24, 33, 50, 66, 75, 97, *151*
Ruby Creek, 90
Russell, Osborne, 28, 35

Salmon, 112
Salmon Fly, *92*
Sandhill cranes, 110
Sandy Mite fly, *150*
Schwiebert, Ernie, *58*, 65, 66, 79, *82*, *85*, 143
Second Meadow (Slough Creek), *viii*, *26*, 28, 32
Sentinel Creek, 64
Seven Mile Bridge (Madison River), 81, *84*, 143
Seven Mile Run (Madison River), 81
Sheepeater Cliffs (Gardner River), *21*, 22
Shoshone Creek, 43
Shoshone Lake, 43, *45*, 50, 139
Shoshone Range, 123
Skunk Hair Caddis fly, 40, 107
Slate Mahogany Dun fly, 121
Slate Wing Olive fly, 120
Slide Inn (Madison River), 16, 90
Slide Inn Run (Madison River), 90, *96*
Slough Creek, *viii*, 9, 16, 27–32, 40
    First Meadow section of, 31–32
    recommended flies for, 32–33
    sections of, 27–28
    wildlife on, 28
Slough Creek Campground, 27
Snake River, 10, 56. *See also* Henry's Fork
Soda Butte Creek, 35, *36*
Sofa Pillow fly, 24, 41, *150*
Solfatara Creek, 69–70
Solfatera Plateau, 69
Sparse Grey Hackle (writer), 120

Speckled Dun and Spinner fly, 120
Spruce Marabou Muddler fly, 50, 87
Spruce streamer fly, 70, 107
Squaw Creek, 90
Stilts, 110
Stream management, 9–11
Sulphur Caldron (Yellowstone River), 124, *125*, 127, 131, *132*

Tackle, 17, 87, 94, 101–104
Tetons Range, 10
Thompson, David, 123
Thorofare Creek, 123
Thorofare Plateau, 123
Three Brothers Peak, 79
Three Forks (town), 99, 109
Three Rivers Peak, 99
Timberline Reclamations Company, 106
Tower Creek, 127
Tower Falls (Yellowstone River), 127
Townsend, Mary Trowbridge, 56
Trout Shop, The (West Yellowstone), 32, 40
Trude fly, *150*
Trumpeter swans, 127, 143

United States Fish and Wildlife Service, 31, 40, 54
Upper Coffee Pot rapids (Henry's Fork), 110
Upper Falls (Yellowstone River), 127
Upper Iron Bridge (Firehole River), 59

Varney (town), 90
Varney Bridge (Madison River), 90, 94
Vint's Special fly, *151*
VIP Pool (Slough Creek), 28, *29*, 31
Virginia Cascades (Gibbon River), *68*, 69
Virginia Meadows (Gibbon River), 69

Waders, 17
Wahl, Ralph, 143
Washburn, Mount, 28
Water ouzel, *20*
Waters of Yellowstone with Rod and Fly, The, (Back), 27, 135, 143
Western Green Drake fly, 79, 97, 120, 130

Western Quill Gordon fly, 41, 130
Westfork (Gallatin River), *103*
West Fork (Madison River), 16, 90
West Fork Bridge (Madison River), 90
West Thumb (town), 16
West Yellowstone (town), 13, 16, 31, 40, 77, 81, 94, 99, 104, 113, 139
Whitefish, 90
White Winged Black fly, 66, 97, 121
White Winged Sulphur Drake fly, 97
Whitlock, Dave, 81
Wilson, Bob, 24
Wilson, Sharman, 24
Wind River Range, 123
Winter, Koke, 94, 113–116
Wolf Creek, 90
Wolf Lake, 69
Woolly Bugger fly, 107, 121
Woolly Worm fly, 22, 131, 151
Wulff, Lee, 133

Yellow Stone fly, 121, 131
Yellowstone Lake, 123
Yellowstone Park, 13, 99, 123
  accomodations in, 13–16
  headquarters of, 16, 22
  Historical Museum and Library of, 16
  regulations in, 133
  wildlife in, 142–143
Yellowstone River, 9, 10, 16, 27, 37, 123, 124–127
  Alum Creek section of, 127
  Black Canyon section of, 127, *128*, 130
  Buffalo Ford section of, 124
  insects life on, 130–131
  recommended flies for, 130–131
  Sulphur Caldron section of, 124, *125*, *132*
  upper, 13
  wildlife on, 127
Yellowstone waters, *14–15* (map)
  climate of, 17
  insect life on, 145–147
  recommended flies for, 148–153
Yosemite National Park, 40
Yount's Peak (Yellowstone River), 123

Zern, Ed, 106
Zug Bug fly, 33, 41